ONE
TO
ONE

MICHAEL GREEN

Author of _Who Is This Jesus?_

O N E
T O
O N E

How to share your faith with a friend

MOORINGS
Nashville, Tennessee
A Division of the Ballantine Publishing Group,
Random House, Inc.

ONE TO ONE: How to Share Your Faith with a Friend

Copyright © 1995 by Michael Green

Library of Congress Catalog Card Number: 95-77330

ISBN: 0-345-40089-5

First American Edition: July 1995

10 9 8 7 6 5 4 3 2 1

Contents

Introduction

Almost all the major churches in the world have agreed to make the 1990s a decade of evangelism. Nobody knows who had the idea first: it seems to have come from God himself, for otherwise it would be hard to see so unpopular an emphasis commending itself to churches across the globe! No longer is *evangelism* a dirty word, reserved for fanatics. It is the declared policy of almost all Christian churches.

As a result evangelism is regularly discussed in church circles. It is hardly possible to have a church meeting without the subject coming up in some shape or form. But rather less is actually being done! People will cheerfully go to a conference on evangelism. They will be less enthusiastic to raise the topic of Jesus Christ even with close friends and colleagues.

This little book is written to help people, ordinary Christian people, get started on what is the most worthwhile and fulfilling ministry any Christian can have, that of introducing someone else to Christ. We do not have to wait for the big crusade to come to town. We do not have to wait for the next evangelistic church service or outreach dinner. Any Christian can talk about the good news to a friend.

A number of factors make this personal approach

very significant, particularly in the present climate. First, there is a great hunger for spirituality today in our society. It may be alternative medicine. It may be witchcraft. It may be ancient paganism. It may be the New Age. But the hunger is there. That provides us with an enormous opportunity that was not there even ten years ago.

Second, there is a good deal of suspicion of organized religion. Jesus is popular; the church is not. That is partly because many people have bad memories of the church: some hurt received, some hypocrisy discerned, some boredom encountered. It is partly because in this postmodern age there is a strong reaction against all the traditional pillars of a life style inherited from the Enlightenment two and a half centuries ago. And rightly or wrongly, the church is seen as part of the established order that people want to get away from. Therefore, taking the opportunity for personal testimony to the joy and reality of Jesus is likely to be more productive than inviting a friend to church, valuable though that can be.

Third, it has been shown by survey after survey that the majority of people come to faith today over a period of time. It is not so much a crisis, more a process. It may well have a critical point in it, but owing to the lack of Christian knowledge today and the generally perceived implausibility of the Christian case, most people take a good while to come around to it. The report, edited by John Finney, called *Finding Faith Today* is a careful survey of the faith journeys of recent converts to Christianity. It shows that out of a broadly based sample of 511 people who had made "a public profession of faith" in the previous twelve months, 69 percent described their coming to faith as gradual. The report comments: "The gradual process is the way in which the majority of people discover God, and the average time taken is about four years. Models of evangelism which help people along the pathway are needed." This book explores one such model.

Fourth, it is abundantly plain that the vast majority of people who come to faith are more influenced by friends or family members than by any other single factor. Church, the Bible, preaching, and visitation are low on the list of attractors; by far the highest is the friendship of a committed, warm, unembarrassed Christian. That seems to be the magnet for some 77 percent of new Christians in the West. So it stands to reason that if we want the gospel to spread, we need to pay enormous attention to the building of relationships and the natural conversation about Jesus that can emerge from the trust those relationships engender.

I have written this book to help Christians approach and talk with their friends about the good news. No knowledge of theology is assumed, no acquired techniques. Personal evangelism is essentially personal; it cannot be too tightly programmed. So my suggestions are open textured. They seek to avoid both the woolly vagueness that marks some talk about evangelism and the narrow dogmatism and strict techniques that mark other approaches. When I wrote *Evangelism Through the Local Church,* a large volume directed primarily toward ministers and leaders in churches, I was asked on several occasions for something short and practical for the ordinary Christian who wanted to know how to go about telling the good news to a friend. That is what I have tried to provide in this unpretentious volume. If it helps you to open your mouth and tell a friend about Jesus, I shall be amply repaid.

Most of the material here comes from a lifetime of experience in talking about the gospel rather than from the many books on the subject. I have reused and adapted some of the material from *Evangelism Through the Local Church* where I thought it appropriate. Some may find it too simple, but that is a good fault for a theologian like me! Far too many Christians think the whole thing is so difficult that they are reluctant to try.

Finally, in this gender-conscious age, I ask the understanding of my women readers if in referring to humankind, I generally stick to the traditional "he" rather than constantly use "he or she," which I find cumbersome. But there is nothing said of a man in this little book on personal evangelism that does not apply equally to a woman. Indeed, women are frequently better at discussing the gospel than men are.

My prayer for us all is that we may be natural—with Jesus Christ just below the surface—and may be ready for him to surface in our conversation when the time is right.

Michael Green

1

Getting Motivated

You could hardly believe it. But there it was in the London *Sunday Times* of August 21, 1994. The Reverend Stephen Abakah, who until recently had been basking on the sun-kissed shores of Cape Coast in Ghana, is joining several hundred missionaries from Third World countries to Britain. They rightly see our country as godless and immoral. They want to work in partnership with British Christians in calling this country back to God. It is a bit of a shock for us to realize that there are more Anglicans in Nigeria than in Europe and North America combined. But it is even more of a shock for these Christians from the Two-Thirds World to come here and discover how godless this country is. There are Peruvian missionaries in Belfast, Indians in York, Nigerians in Manchester, Sri Lankans in Widnes, Egyptians in Middlesbrough, Brazilians in Edinburgh, and Liberians in Plymouth. We are returning to spread Christianity back to the West, said Luis Beldeon from Peru. "We must reintroduce Christianity to the masses," said Stephen Abakah. "We in Africa are grateful to British missionaries for bringing us Christianity, but now I think it is Britain that needs our help. It is time to remind people about the gospel and ask them why they are turning away from God."

These missionaries are puzzled at two levels. First, because they were led to believe that the West is Christian, and they come here and find that it is nothing of the kind. As one of them put it, "It seems to be possible to believe in absolutely nothing in [the West]: not Christianity, not Islam, not Hinduism. It can be a big shock for missionaries arriving here and finding people and areas that are totally godless." I can't argue with that, can you?

The second reason for their amazement is the feeble defensiveness and indefensible apathy of the church members in this country. They are amazed by the low spiritual life and lack of zeal among us. "Churches here are not as lively as they are in Ghana," said Abakah with masterly tact and understatement. I can't argue with that, either.

So these courageous Christians, reversing the events of a century ago, when Victorian Christians went worldwide to preach the gospel, are coming to a godless country to help us bring our country back to the living God.

And they *are* very courageous. Take someone like Sung Hee Kwong, who left a highly paid job in Seoul, South Korea, to come to South London in 1985, when she spoke only a few words of English. She gives out leaflets on the streets of Streatham and talks about Jesus to people walking in the parks. She sets up a Christian stall in a fair near her home. She has good news to tell—which she was blind to in her Buddhist days. It is all about the life-changing power of Jesus Christ. It is hardly surprising that she now numbers seventy people in her Christian worship groups.

If Christians from overseas care enough to help us, should we not be doing something about it ourselves? It may seem difficult, but it brings immense joy when we see others join the Christian family and discover the reality of Jesus in their lives. Someone like Norman, for instance, a worker on the factory floor in a north-country mill town. He discovered Jesus through friendship with Tim, a fellow worker. Tim invited him along to hear Billy Graham on one of his recent visits to Britain and helped him to get settled in as a Christian after he had gone forward and committed himself at the crusade meeting. That was a great joy. But it did not end there. Norman's father, Walter, another factory worker, could not help noticing the difference in his son's life. So he got interested. He had many a long talk with Tim and came to his wedding. At the reception Tim's dad happened to meet Walter and had the joy of helping him to make his personal decision for Christ. Before long Walter's wife, too, came to the Lord, and they both got involved at church. Meanwhile Norman had introduced his wife to Jesus; soon he was leading the youth group in the church, and she has become a local church leader! They then came across another coworker who had spent time in prison, and before long he, too, was rejoicing in the friendship of Jesus Christ. Guess what he is doing now. Running a halfway house for ex-addicts and prisoners!

Look at the new network of Christian relationships that has grown in that tough northern town. Look at what it has done in the homes, in the factory, and in reaching out to some of the neediest people in society. And look at the factors that brought them to Christ. There was the vibrant, informed faith of Tim. There was the quality of his Christian life, which excited comment. There were the friendships he developed. There was the very natural invitation to Norman to accompany him to hear Billy Graham. There was the steady nurture after a decision. There was the joy of one telling another, in the family and beyond. There was the impact of the church. There was the joy of the wedding and the unplanned talk that led to Walter's commitment. A whole variety of factors went into the reversal of godless attitudes that is now underway in the town, the very reversal that our overseas visitors want to promote. It's a tremendous joy. It's clearly what we should be doing if we have found Jesus as the pearl of great price. They call it *evangelism*. It means "spreading good news."

EVANGELISM—NO THANKS!

The whole idea of evangelism is unfamiliar to many churchpeople and objectionable to others. That is understandable. After all, the Christian faith has been around for a long time. It has shaped much of the culture of four continents. Churches are to be found in every town and village. The vast majority of people in England and North America would describe themselves as Christians rather than as members of any other religion. Many of them have been baptized as infants. So where does evangelism fit in? Are we not all Christians, especially if we are born in a "Christian" country? The whole idea of evangelism seems strange and unnecessary.

Many churchpeople feel more strongly than that. Evangelism is very unattractive to them. They have mental pictures of televangelists frothing at the mouth with impassioned appeals, first for your soul and then for your money. And more than one of these televangelists has been notorious for financial or sexual misconduct. No, the whole idea is reprehensible. In any case, is not evangelism a sort of brainwashing just like what goes on in the cults? Why not let people make up their own minds on things like religion and values? This is a pluralistic age after all. Why should anyone try to change another person's beliefs and allegiance?

EVANGELISM—WHAT DID JESUS THINK OF IT?

That all sounds fine until we see what the Founder of Christianity has to say on the subject. He was far from regarding all churchpeople or religious people as in the clear. He lived among passionately dedicated worshipers of the one true God, the God who had revealed himself in Scripture. They gave a tenth of their income to God's work, had a very high respect for their clergy, tried to regulate their lives by the teachings of their faith, went regularly to synagogue, and above all had a tremendous devotion to the temple at Jerusalem. Yet he had to tell them they would never enter—indeed, never *see*—the kingdom of God unless they repented of their sinful attitudes, entrusted their lives to him, and became his disciples. He went to great lengths in his teaching to make it plain that he was the way to God, the final truth about God, and the very life of God incarnate. Listen to this, for example: "All things have been committed to me by my Father. No one knows the Son except the Father, and no one knows the Father except the Son and those to whom the Son chooses to reveal him" (Matt. 11:27).

What an amazing claim! Only Jesus really knows the Father. Only he can make him known. He then issues a staggering invitation. Not "Come to the Law" or "Come to the temple," but "Come to me, all you who are weary and burdened, and I will give you rest." He does not invite them to take upon themselves what the Jews called "the yoke of the law," but says, "Take my yoke upon you and learn from me, for I am gentle and humble in heart, and you will find rest for your souls" (Matt. 11:28–29).

Jesus reinforced this strong emphasis on his mission and person in the parables. He told about the lost coin, the lost sheep, the lost son. The thrust of stories like these is twofold. First, to show that we human beings are lost. And second, to show that God is full of love for us and prepared to go to any lengths to get us back. If we are to take Jesus seriously, we are far from all right as we are, however Christian the country we live in—and who would claim that for any country in Europe or North America?

Jesus is just as dismissive of the idea that we do not need to engage in evangelism. The televangelists may get it wrong, but that does not let us off the hook. No sooner did he assemble a band of disciples than he took them out preaching with him. Then he sent them out on their own. Subsequently, he sent seventy others to get on with the job of proclaiming the kingdom of God and living lives that showed the kingdom had arrived. His final instructions to his disciples were to "go and make disciples of all nations," and he promised his abiding presence and power only to those who obeyed that injunction (Matt. 28:18–20).

In the light of the Founder's instructions, it is hard to see how Christians can properly duck out of evangelism.

EVANGELISM—WHY BOTHER?

Even so, we naturally shy away from evangelism. For one thing, we are not quite sure what it is. For another, is it not the pastor's job? And anyhow, we ought not to invade someone else's private space or to try and persuade people to change their minds about personal matters. In any case, we feel we don't know enough; we might make a mess of it and put them off forever.

Such thoughts run through our minds when we think (occasionally) about evangelism. I am sure God understands them because he has given some very powerful motivations to encourage us to be up and doing.

For one thing, God himself is the supreme evangelist. All through the Bible he is portrayed as the God who loves us even when we rebel against him. Indeed, "God so loved the world that he gave his one and only Son, that whoever believes in him shall not perish but have eternal life" (John 3:16). If God is like that, surely something of his loving concern should rub off on us, his worshipers?

For another, Jesus displayed a constant and profound care for those he called "lost," lost in loneliness, separation from God, defeat, lack of purpose. He was always reaching out to them with the evangel, or good news, of the possibility of rescue and restoration once they entered the kingdom of God. That kingdom is not a place; it is a relationship with the King. It is a matter of putting God in his rightful place as number one in life. That is what Jesus was calling people to do; and as they responded, they became welded into a sort of new society—a counterculture composed of people who not only talked of God's kingly rule but displayed it in their lives and relationships. Through his preaching, through his healings and exorcisms, Jesus made it plain that he had come to bring in this kingdom of God. And at the end of his life on earth, as we have seen, he commissioned his followers to continue the job of proclaiming the good news and calling on people to respond. The last wishes of a dear friend are a sacred trust, are they not? How much more so is the last command of Jesus?

The Holy Spirit was the parting gift of Jesus to his people. The main purpose of the Spirit's coming was to equip them for the mission that they would otherwise have found too difficult. The disciples were expressly told not to go out of Jerusalem and try evangelizing in their own strength, but to await the gift of the Spirit, who would enable them to bear courageous and effective witness (Acts 1:8).

How could there be a stronger motivation than this? The whole triune God whom we worship, Father, Son, and Holy Spirit, is deeply concerned with evangelism. If we take our Christianity seriously, how can we hold back?

But there are two other considerations to bear in mind as we wonder whether to get involved in this good news business. One is the fact that we are entrusted by God with the gospel. After all, whom can he use to be messengers of reconciliation apart from those who have themselves been reconciled? How can he use people, however talented, who are still holding out against his love? Clearly, he can't. That's why the New Testament talks about our being Christ's ambassadors, his messengers, his stewards, his heralds, his servants, his witnesses. He relies on us. Indeed, he has no other way of extending the bounds of his kingdom than through the agency of those who are already members of it. It is an awesome privilege to represent the living God. And it is a compelling motive, too. The other thing to bear in mind is that people without Christ are in real need. This need is soft-pedaled in our permissive society, which loosely assumes that it does not matter what you believe. All will be well in the end. Jesus assures us that this is not the case. He tells us that we are either members of his kingdom or outside its gates. We are either reconciled with God or rebels. We are either lost or found. We are either in the wedding feast or in outer darkness. We are either building our lives on the rock of Jesus and his teaching or else building on sand. We are either for him or against him. We are either sheep or goats. We are either on the bonfire or in the barn. We are either on the broad way that leads to destruction or on the narrow way that leads to life. That is the human condition, according to Jesus. We are in deep need of Jesus the great physician, Jesus the reconciler, Jesus the sacrifice for sins, Jesus the bridge between God and man. We have either thrown in our lot with him or not. It is a clear choice. There is no middle ground. Of course, there is plenty of room for gradual movement from darkness to light: it does not have to be a blinding flash and an immediate decision. Nevertheless, none of us can escape this change of masters. None of us can avoid bowing the knee to ask for forgiveness and reinstatement in the family of God.

Very well then. What of those who have not yet come to that point? They are in real need. Either they are, as Paul puts it, "without hope and without God in the world" (Eph. 2:12), or else "they are ignorant of the righteousness that comes from God and seek to establish their own" (Rom. 10:3, author's translation). Of course, they do not see it like that; and Paul has an explanation for that, too. He is well aware, from much personal experience, that there is a great outside hindrance to evangelism, the devil. He calls him "the god of this age," who takes God's place in people's hearts. And, says Paul, he has "blinded the minds of unbelievers, so that they cannot see the light of the gospel of the glory of Christ." Paul's strategy, in response to this, is a life that shines with the renewing power of Christ, fearless witness to "Jesus Christ as Lord" and, by implication, heartfelt prayer to "God, who said, 'Let light shine out of darkness,'" that he will "shine in our hearts to give us the light of the knowledge of the glory of God in the face of Christ" (2 Cor. 4:1–6). A holy life, fervent prayer, and fearless witness: that is how people who are blinded by enemy propaganda may be brought to see the truth they need so desperately.

So our responsibility and people's need are two additional motives to rouse us from our apathy. But let us not go away feeling it is all a matter of dull duty. It isn't. To help someone else to discover Jesus Christ is the greatest joy on earth. We are told there is joy in heaven over one sinner who repents. Well, there is joy on earth, too. Here's an example that reached me only yesterday:

> The highlight of our visit to Israel was having dinner together each evening, when one of us shared a poem on his spiritual journey. One man, Jackson, shared his in the midst of the rich fellowship of a French restaurant. While he was speaking, we became deeply moved by the presence of our Lord, and none of us could speak. Later I asked Jackson to give the poem to the owner of the restaurant. She came back, having read it, with tears in her eyes. "I've never read anything with this kind of spirituality in it before. This is beautiful!" Katie said. She was crying. Then Jackson and I sang a duet of Psalm 25 we learned in our old Stanford days. The whole restaurant came unglued, and we had an amazing time sharing the Lord until 1 A.M. I thought of you that night, envisioning you on the piano bench . . . preaching the gospel. Each night was a new adventure in another restaurant, sharing the joy of the Lord with waiters and waitresses.

Nothing dull or embarrassing about that!

BUT PERSONAL EVANGELISM?

"Very well. Evangelism is part of the church's responsibility," you may be saying. "But there are lots of different ways of evangelism, and in any case it is the pastor's job."

Both statements are true, and both are misleading. It is true that there are lots of different ways of evangelism. Some people come to faith through going to a church service; some through reading a portion of the

Bible; some through a vision; some through a healing; some through a sermon; some through something they read. But extensive modern research in various countries leaves us in no doubt that *most people are brought to faith through the loving persistence and friendship of someone close to them:* a spouse, a friend, a family member. Remember Norman, Walter, and their wives!

The actual step of commitment may be brought about through a sermon or an evangelistic rally, but the real work, preparing the way for the gospel, has already been done by that friend or relative through love, prayer, consistent living, and gracious, appropriate testimony. That is why personal evangelism is so crucial. Our circle of friends and acquaintances is unique. Nobody else has the relationship with that circle that we have. We are the Lord's representatives to them. The New Testament has some interesting ways of suggesting how that role of representative might work out. It sees each of us as a sweet fragrance of Christ, like a woman's perfume or the attractive aroma of bread baking in the kitchen. It sees us as willing captives in Christ's triumphal procession. It sees us as open letters that anyone can read. It sees us as witnesses, willing and able to tell what we have seen and experienced. Yes, there are lots of ways of evangelism, but none is so compelling, none so effective, as the meeting of friends, the conversation of those who know and trust one another.

Personal evangelism is the best sort of evangelism. I recall Billy Graham saying just that years ago, when I was a student at Cambridge University. Hundreds of theological students were at breakfast, and he was the speaker. He was aware that many were skeptical about the value of crusade evangelism, which was new to England at that time. And I recall his saying something like this: "Mass evangelism is not the best way of evangelism, but it seems to be the way that God has entrusted to me, and I must be faithful to it. The best way of evangelism is when there are two people talking together and one leads the other to Jesus."

Just as politics is too important to leave to the politicians, so evangelism is too important to leave to the clergy. The pastor may know more than you do, but he will not have your circle of friends. He will never be able to meet them as naturally as you can. They will probably be unwilling to come clean with him in the way they do with you. He will be seen as the professional who has a line to promote; you are the amateur who has no axe to grind. No, you can't leave it to the pastor, however good an evangelist he may be. "The body does not consist of one member but of many" (1 Cor. 12:14 NRSV), and we all have a part to play in spreading the good news. Our friends who are not yet Christians need to see that this good news is really good for us. It makes a difference in our lives, and we are not embarrassed to commend it in our own words.

Two examples brought this home to me, and they will always stay in my mind. One was when a group of students went off to run a summer holiday for youngsters with disabilities. On their return I asked them if there had been any professions of conversion. They replied, "Yes, there was one." When I asked which of them had been instrumental in that change of direction, the answer came back, "Oh, it was none of us. It was a girl so badly disabled that she could only speak about five words a minute. She was the one who led her friend to Christ."

The other was an older woman of, I think, ninety-six. She was in the hospital, and when I, her pastor, went to visit her, I heard her talking in a loud voice to the doctor who was in attendance and challenging him about his relationship with God. When she saw me, she said, "Oh, here's Michael. He can tell you more about it."

We are all members of Christ's body. Each member has a job to do. That job includes personal witness to Jesus.

2

Building Bridges

If you go for a vacation in Wales or Scotland, you cannot help being struck by the large number of castles, many of them now in ruins. In medieval days the castle was the place of control over the surrounding countryside, the place to run into and be safe when there was an enemy attack. It seems to me that the Christian church in the West is in danger of going back to the castle culture. It used to control public life, especially in matters of honesty, relationships, education, law, medicine, peace, and war. That control has long since gone. However, Christians are in the habit of retiring into the castle of the church—its customs, its dress, its attitudes.

But there is a growing alienation between the people in the castle and the people outside it; the gap between Christians and others is growing all the time. The climate is cold out there in secular society, with materialism, violence, sexual abuse, relativism, and the like. So it is only natural to seek the shelter of churchy people and pursuits; that is where we feel safe. But we must resist this very natural tendency. Our place is not to be in the castle, but to be in the world; "in the world but not of it" was how Jesus expressed it.

If we opt for a castle culture, we can be sure of this:

it will become a ruin. A Christianity that does not give itself away to others will die. You see that happening all the time in churches where a small and shrinking congregation insists on music, liturgy, dress, language, and habits that are quite alien to secular neighbors. So people who are not yet Christians don't just have to face up to the challenge of Jesus; they are asked to take on board a new, and frankly unattractive, culture.

But what a difference when the castle community, instead of locking itself away with raised drawbridge, lowered portcullis, and full moat, opens itself up to the people out there! When the traffic flows both ways, and the castle, bright with flags and bunting, invites the locals in to a feast in the great hall. What a difference when the portcullis is raised, the drawbridge is down, and there is a natural mingling of castle dwellers and the rest. That is what we need to work for if we are to introduce people to the Lord of the castle and encourage them to join his retinue.

To put it another way, many Christian churches these days are like a ghetto in one of our big cities—a community of immigrants in a foreign country, clinging together for warmth and understanding, and surrounded by a society that does not understand or seem to care. When churches have become like this, their biggest need is to get out of the ghetto and to give up forever the ghetto mentality. *We have to build bridges!*

BUILDING BRIDGES TO PEOPLE

Many churches have never learned to build bridges even within the church itself! Many churchpeople have no idea what others in the congregation do with their leisure time. There is not much social interaction in the homes of the people; there are not many occasional gatherings in a living room with a few friends to pray.

The church may be likened in the Bible to a building, but a church like this is a building without any cement between the bricks. It may be likened to a body, but a church like this is a body with many detached limbs.

But once there is some sort of bridge building within the church itself, it is much easier to build bridges to the people who live in the locality. Many churches have never looked at the demographics of their area, so they do not know what the needs are. Consequently, they cannot gauge their activities toward trying to meet those needs. And even when such an attempt is made, there is still a crying need to make the church and its activities user-friendly. If we, as churches, have good news to share, we simply have to be in the bridge-building business. All our church activities should have an outward orientation.

If that is true for the church at large, it is even more essential for the individual who wants to help others to faith. We simply must escape from the endless run of meetings where Christians talk to themselves, and get out among people who are still strangers to Jesus. When churches are vibrating with life, they do not have a lot of organized midweek activities. Members are expected to use their leisure time to make friends and build relationships that can become bridges to Jesus. But when churches have lost that zeal, all manner of midweek activities emerge—the task of the church has unconsciously changed from reaching unbelievers to entertaining the Christians! I recall hearing about a series of lifeboat stations formed years ago on the east coast of the United States. They were rough-and-ready structures, but they harbored tough, durable lifeboats manned by intrepid sailors who would risk life and limb to rescue shipwrecked mariners. But over the course of time, the lifeboat stations turned into marinas. Nobody went out on rescue missions any-more. People went sailing instead. That is like the softening of resolve and action that has debilitated many a church, many an individual. It has to be changed.

Changing it is not difficult, once we see ourselves not as yachtsmen but as a lifeboat crew.

We all have *relatives*. It is hard to be an ambassador of Christ to them—they know us and our weaknesses so well. But it can be done. I know many children who have been led to Christ by their parents. I know many parents who have been so amazed by the transformation in their children that they have had the humility to turn to Christ themselves. I know many men and women who have been loved and prayed into faith by their partners. I know many people who attribute their conversion to the faithful prayers of a relative, maybe a grandmother. "Life before lip" is the basic motto if you want to influence relatives for Christ. Then introduce as many attractive Christians to them as you can. Keep praying. And look for opportunities, maybe for yourself, but perhaps for someone else to come into the situation and reap where you have sown.

We all have *friends*. We are ideally situated to be ambassadors of Christ to them. Here again prayer, intentional prayer for them personally, is essential. So is an attractive life, surrendered to Jesus at every conscious point. But it is also important actually to talk to our friends about the Lord, as and when opportunity offers, for the simple reason that they will take things from us that they will not take from anyone else. As friends, we have earned the right to speak. And so when we invite them to some occasion when the good news of Christ is going to be made clear, they are likely to accept—not because they want to go, but because they want to please the friend who has invited them. So often we fail our friends by withholding from them the element that could take our friendship to the deepest of all levels. We do not tell them about the most important aspect of our own lives, our relationship with Jesus, nor do we commend Christ to them with all the enthusiasm of personal discovery. Jesus longs for us to try to introduce our friends to him, the Friend who sticks closer than a brother.

Many of us have *fellow workers*—or, if we are unemployed, colleagues who are in the same situation and show up at the same unemployment line. A certain bonding takes place simply by being alongside folks in the same situation as ourselves. Christians need reminding that their main sphere of Christian service is not Sundays and what they do in voluntary church work in the evenings; their job is their main sphere of Christian ministry. It is here that their witness does or does not cut ice.

It is our life style that makes the difference among our coworkers. I think of Mick, ordained now, who spent twenty years on the shop floor, and how the warmth of his personality, the gentleness of his language, the thoroughness with which he did the job, and his care for and interest in his coworkers drew many of them to talk with him and ask the secret of a life like that. He led many of them to Jesus—so many that in the end he became a minister and did it full-time, so to speak! I think of my own son, now a missionary overseas, who spent some years working first on the shop floor and then as a manager in a factory. His dealing with the men at work, his entertaining of them in his home, and his visiting them when they were sick made a profound impact. They had never met a manager like that. His life style sprang from his relationship with Jesus. And it showed.

We all have *leisure interests*. They throw us into contact with other people who share our interests and are therefore open to an approach from us. It does not matter whether your leisure interest is listening to country music, collecting butterflies, or fishing. Nothing is too bizarre to provide opportunity to talk with others who enjoy the same thing. The interest we share *is* the bridge; we hardly need to do any building.

Then pause to think of the people whose *lives inter-sect with yours:* the garbage collector, the mail carrier, the store clerk, the neighbors down the street, the man who walks his dog past your house. All these people have lives that intersect, to some degree, with your own. Do they not need the good news of Jesus that you enjoy? Opportunity may well open up for you to say something to them. It can happen in the most unexpected way. At the school entrance. In the Laundromat. In the checkout line. I think of an occasion when I got into the deepest of conversations about Jesus with an Irish poacher as we stood at dead of night on a sandbank in an estuary trying to net salmon!

Sometimes we get opportunities when the intersection is marginal. A friend of mine went to pray for a colleague who was ill. When he emerged, a woman of about seventy was complaining about where he had parked his car. He was very courteous to her and was invited in. Within an hour or two, he had led her to Christ. And then her husband came in; she told him, and he burst out in praise to God, for he had been praying for her for a great many years! You never know what opportunities may come your way if you are willing for the Lord to use you as his ambassador. That makes each day an adventure!

BUILDING BRIDGES TO GOD

Building bridges to people leads naturally into something even more important: building bridges to God. Of course, if we are Christians at all, the bridge has already been constructed by the coming and dying and rising of Jesus, and we have crossed it. But we live a good deal of our lives without giving the Lord a thought. It is a sort of self-induced isolation. And it shows in three main ways.

First, there is the failure to build bridges in *prayer*. This is one of the main ways in which Western Christianity is distinguished from African, Asian, and Latin-American expressions of the faith. We rely on technology, on books, videos, organization—in a word, on making things happen. They are often deprived of these props, which is a good thing because it makes them rely on *God* to make things happen. Thus, you find the level of faith, the commitment to prayer, and the practice of fasting infinitely more developed in these continents than in our own. It is no surprise that the gospel is spreading much faster and deeper there than it is in Western churches. For God loves to answer prayer. He loves to have his children seek his face with their needs. He has made the most marvelous promises in Scripture for those who fast and pray. He invites us to come and share with him our concern for our friends, knowing that his concern for them is far greater. Alas, the words of James are highly relevant to our virtually prayerless Western church: "You do not have, because you do not ask God" (James 4:2).

Where do we find the nights of prayer in our Western churches that are commonplace in Africa and Asia? Where do we find the seriousness of purpose that is prepared to go without food for days in order the better to meet with God? It is very rare. Yes, let's be specific. Are there people *you* are praying for daily? People for whom you beseech God with intensity and fasting? That is the first step to seeing them won to Christ. It never happens without prayer. And funnily enough, the person concerned is usually aware of it. I frequently ask individuals who have just come to faith who they think has been praying for them. They generally know!

Our second failure to build bridges to God comes in

the area of *ignorance*. God has given us the Scriptures to make his way of salvation very plain. He expects his servants to know their way about them. We do not need to be budding theologians, but it helps to have a working knowledge of the main road, so to speak, back to God. How can we explain it to others if we are not clear about it ourselves? And many churchpeople are not at all clear about it. They have been in church all their lives and have heard countless sermons, but they are quite unprepared to explain to others who are seeking how they can get right with God. That can even apply to the clergy, who are rarely trained in personal evangelism in their theological colleges.

You need not feel this is a massive challenge to your understanding and memory. You can begin with just one verse, such as John 3:16. You can then add a few verses as you come across them, make a note of them in the back of your Bible, and have them ready when opportunity knocks. Many Christians have a time of prayer on a regular daily basis, a time when they read a dozen verses or so of Scripture. Well, if instead of doing that, you read one verse (and its reference so that you can find it again easily) a dozen times, you will know it, and you can add it to your collection. We will return to this subject in a later chapter. For the moment, it is important, in this age so ignorant of the world's bestseller, to build bridges to its central teaching on how men and women can get right with God.

Our third failure to build bridges to God is very widespread. We do not *keep in touch* with him, or "abide in him," as John 15 puts it. We know how a branch abides in a tree and so can bear fruit. We know how a baby can abide in her mother's arms, and so find security and warmth and love. But we do not make a habit of practicing the presence of God. We do not often pause during the events of the day to look up into his face and tell him we love him. But the people

God uses most are those who keep in closest touch with him. I can think of times when I have been in that situation and have sensed his nudge to go and talk to someone. To my amazement, when I have done so, I have often found that person open to talk and keen to find out about God. Like Lydia at Philippi, here is a person whose heart the Lord opened (Acts 16:14), and I would have missed the opportunity if I had not been consciously in touch with Jesus. I dread to think of the opportunities I constantly miss through my failure to keep close. It is only as we abide in him that we bear any fruit at all. It is literally true that without him we can do nothing. John 15 is a crucial passage to ponder if we want to be any use to God in helping others to discover him.

Bridge building is indispensable.

3

Starting the Conversation

Years ago there was a saying in World Council of Churches' circles that was open to misinterpretation, but contained a lot of truth: "Let the world set the agenda." As a description of what Christian concerns should be, it left a lot to be desired. But as a wise approach to the variety of people we meet, it has much to commend it. If you want to open up a good conversation about Jesus, then let the folks you are talking to set the scene. It will be more helpful and natural that way. People are so varied, and their interests, starting points, and needs are so diverse, that it is asking for trouble to barge in with some premeditated sermonette or some technique learned from a book about the best way to approach people. After all, we are individuals, and we do not appreciate being treated as if we were just some sample human specimens, ripe to be evangelized!

Very likely the entry point will emerge through some situation where a friend of ours is brought up against painful reality and does not know quite where to turn. It may be a broken engagement. It may be experiencing a divorce in the family, losing a job, or suddenly discovering she is adopted. It may be the death of a dear one; I am involved in precisely that situation as I write.

A neighbor, with whom we have been friendly but not by any means close, has just lost his wife—and he has asked me to officiate at the funeral.

So just think of the appropriate way for you to begin, in each of the common human situations I have outlined.

Where there has been a divorce or a broken engagement, the Lord who is a husband to his people, the friend who will never jilt you, is a natural approach. And how do we know that Jesus' love is like that and can be trusted? Because he came to look for us. Because he went to the cross to die for us. That's why.

The faithfulness of the Lord, who will never let us down and never give us up, is an enormous encouragement to people who have felt the lash of human rejection. What if they have just lost a job? I think the love that Jesus expressed in practical terms to those whom society had marginalized in his day is a firm pledge that he will never fire any of us from his family business. I would major on promises that underline this in both Old and New Testaments—and I would do my best to show practical care, including food and shelter, to a friend in that situation. How can people be expected to believe the love and care of the Lord if his professed followers do not show both characteristics?

Or think of the person who suddenly discovers that she is adopted. It is a tremendous shock, and we need to be alongside in support, listening and loving and not necessarily saying anything much for a while. But when it is time to talk, the New Testament offers breathtaking encouragement, for it takes the *adoption* word and tells us that is what God has done for us. We were lost and homeless, and God has adopted us into his family alongside Jesus. Jesus is child by right; we are adopted children by sheer generosity. That thought can mean so much to those who are a bit down in the mouth about their adopted status.

And what of the person hit by bereavement? Well, here again we need two ears and one mouth. The shock of bereavement is often so great that a friend needs to talk about the dead loved one a lot and is incapable of taking much in. But the time for that will come. And then the gospel has two very special things to offer. One is the companionship of the only person in all the world who has broken the back of death—the risen Jesus Christ. And the other is the fellowship of the Christian family that, if it is offered sensitively and appropriately in the days and months after the funeral, can lead to the bereaved person discovering the truths about God that had previously seemed so obscure. I know many people who have come to a living faith through the door of bereavement.

Often, then, our opportunities will come when we have built a good relationship with a friend, and then some particular situation arises in which we can be a help.

But what if there is no such situation? How are we to open up things then? This is an area many Christians find particularly difficult. It seems so odd, so difficult, so embarrassing to talk about Jesus—just like that. But consider what is at stake. Many of our friends live in a world that is to all intents and purposes atheistic. Even if they theoretically believe in him, theirs is a world from which God has effectively been banished. They never give him a thought. Just reflect on the implications of a world without God.

A WORLD WITHOUT GOD

It is *a world without love.* Of course, people enjoy love and friendships, but they are all in the last analysis illusory; they do not spring from any "love that makes the world go 'round." How can love be a real part of a

materialistic and unfeeling universe? Though most
people don't have the courage to draw the conclusion
so honestly, they would have to agree with Steve Tur-
ner's short poem:

> My love
>> she said
>> that when all's considered
>> we're only machines.
> I chained
>> her to my bedroom wall
>> for future use
>> and she cried.

Notice the logic—and the anguish—of a rigorously
atheistic worldview.

It is also *a world without values*. Here again, of
course, we all have some values, but they are not absolute, not a firm part of the world we live in. They are
subjective, relative. You can pick and choose. Values
must inevitably be arbitrary in a world that has no
moral source, no Creator. Sartre saw this clearly: "If
God does not exist, man is in consequence forlorn. For
he cannot find anything to depend on either inside or
outside himself. . . . Morals are for us both unavoid-
able and impossible." So relativism reigns supreme.

The world of contemporary godlessness is also *a
world without meaning*. The universe sprang from nothing and will return to nothing in due course. The Big
Bang might easily not have happened. The world and
everything in it have neither design nor meaning. People feel this lack of meaning very acutely. It is a major
cause of depression and suicide. Ronald Conway, one
of Australia's leading psychiatrists, put it succinctly
when he said, "Australians have everything, and yet
they have nothing to live for." Friedrich Nietzsche, before him, had written, "Everything lacks meaning. The

goal is lacking. There is no answer to our 'Why?' " He was perfectly correct if there is no God.

It is also *a world without freedom*. Naturally, we prize freedom, but it is ultimately illusory. If there is no personal Creator, we are either a chance collocation of atoms or else chemically determined. Chance or Necessity—that is how the ancient Greeks saw the only possibilities in a godless world, and they were right. As the group Pink Floyd sang, "You're just another brick in the wall."

It is *a world without fulfillment*. People are hungry for something, even though they may not know what it is. Education does not fill that void, nor does success, money, or sex. Sophia Loren spoke for more than Hollywood film stars when she admitted, "In my life there is an emptiness it is impossible to fill."

It is *a world without truth*. Objective truth, which people used to believe in, has been dissolved for most of us into relativism. How often have you heard, "Well, it may be true for you, but it isn't true for me"? Truth has disappeared from the intellectual map into mysticism or syncretism. The law of noncontradiction is ignored; a thing can now be true and not true at the same time. It is hardly surprising that many people resort to the trip within: the drug culture, the New Age, or one of the new cults constantly arising. To be sure, the coinage of truth is still in common use. But it is devalued. It is just paper money. There is no gold standard to which it corresponds.

It is *a world without hope*. Deep down, people have little hope for the future. Starvation, arms industries, wars, urban violence, corruption, lies, pornography, rape of the environment, massive population growth, and terrifying biological engineering scarcely encourage optimism. At a more personal level, our lives are going downhill—and all that awaits them at the end is extinction, like the flame of a candle. The only immortality available is a few years borrowed from the doctors, a cats' home you could endow, or the hope you may be remembered by your family and friends. Even Churchill died saying, "There is no hope." In their hearts, most people tend to agree.

I am not suggesting for a moment that all your friends are atheists or that they all draw the logical consequences of leaving God out of account. None of us can cope with very much truth at a time. And we are all inconsistent. What I am saying is that these consequences follow inexorably if there is no God. And whether that is their basic conviction or not, a large number of modern people live as if there is no God. For all practical purposes, he is discarded. God is not a plausible hypothesis, not a fashionable concept in today's society. And it is important to remember this if you are going to try and help your friend to Christ. He or she will have to swim against the tide. And you had better understand the pull of the tide if you intend to engage in lifesaving!

A CHRISTIAN APPRAISAL

It is very important to understand the way modern society is moving if we are to help modern unchurched people discover Jesus Christ.

In my lifetime, people's responses to faith have changed. I think I can identify three different attitudes of mind. Each of them demands a different approach.

TRUTH

The first was the issue of truth. Back in the fifties the big questions about Christianity were often the intellectual ones. Was Christianity credible in the face of Marxism? Could you believe in God these days? Was Jesus more than man? Did he really rise from the dead?

And if you were able to show good reasons for the Christian case in response to questions like these, you could expect a steady flow of people coming to Christian commitment.

RELEVANCE

Increasingly, however, that approach has become less successful. The apologetics of someone like Josh McDowell, giving firm answers based on the main points of Christian doctrine, began to leave people cold. "Jesus rose from the dead, did he? OK, I believe you, but so what?" People began to worship at the shrine of relevance. It was not truth that was the main stumbling block, but the question of whether Christianity made any difference—to sex, money, old age, ambition, loneliness, world hunger, and the like. That question is still uppermost in many people's minds, but I believe we have now moved on to another stage, and if we do not understand it, we shall not be very good at discerning where a friend's spiritual roots are likely to be.

FEELING

Today, the question is not so much "Is it true?" or even "Does it work?" but "Does it feel good?" Part of the impact of postmodernism, which dissolves truth into subjectivity, is to make us preoccupied with our feelings. Look at New Age emphases: largely on feelings. Look at the commercials on TV: they are assailing your feelings. Look at a British government, or an American president, succeeding perhaps in many policies, but failing hopelessly to bring about in the country the coveted feel-good factor. Without it each sinks relentlessly in the polls. If we neglect this important understanding of where people are in the nineties, we are going to miss out on some wonderful opportunities to help them.

To approach people through their feelings, a way that was almost taboo in the fifties, is not wrong. We do not pretend that feelings are the most important things; they are merely the most important to them at present. If they feel good about the gospel we present to them, they are going to want to find out if it works and if it is true! It is simply the wise starting point for reaching many modern people.

IMPLICATIONS

If this is the case, it may well mean rethinking a lot of our traditional approaches in evangelism. People will not be very responsive to the idea of reading books, but they may feel good about looking at a video. They may not be very responsive to a sermon, but they may be deeply moved by dance, drama, and music in a holistic type of presentation. Evangelical Christians are often suspicious of ceremony, color, incense, and so on in worship, but these elements may provide just the way in for your friend to sense, through inner feelings, something of the reality of God. I think of the "Thomas Mass" that is making such inroads in Finland. It is an astonishing mixture of all traditions of music, preaching, the use of icons, incense, testimony, prayers (both uttered and written before being left on the altar), culminating in the Eucharist. This service is deliberately intended for nonchurchgoers, and it is drawing shoals of them into Christian commitment. Willow Creek Community Church in the Chicago area has gained notoriety for its efforts to reach those who have given up on the traditional church. The "Nine-o-Clock Service" for unchurched youths in Sheffield, England, is held in a nightclub, with dance music, a lot of noise, little light, no preaching, and the message coming over in images on the TV screens all around the hall. The sheer impact draws young people into seeking after Christ and finding him, as the leaders befriend and talk with them later in the week.

Others are finding retreats a way into searching after God; it is hardly surprising that in the frenetic pace of life today retreats in monasteries have never been more popular. Another way of reaching the feelings is through an extended exposure to nature, especially near mountains and the sea. Yet another is to draw your friend into helping people who are in need, hungry, or disabled. I think of previously agnostic young people being moved to tears by becoming part of a relief trip to Eastern Europe with food and medicine given in the name of Christ.

This may seem strange to us if we have been nourished on a diet of sound doctrine and rational, linear thinking. But we must sit where they sit, and many people today operate more on their feelings of what is acceptable and good than on any other principle. We certainly cannot blame them in an age when pluralism, relativism, and the denial of objective truths form the background of the culture in which they are reared. Such a climate fosters the trip within! Today, the feelings are often the most important way in which to begin a useful conversation about Jesus with your friends.

A CHRISTIAN APPROACH

Very well then. How are we to start up a conversation? There is no one particular way. We have to be true to our own nature, our own way of expressing things, our own relationship with that friend. But there are, perhaps, some general things that may be said.

First, we need to speak with *modesty*. The world is

too full of brash people who are always trying to sell us something. They are hard, pushy, and unattractive. We shy away from them—and quite right, too. People will shy away from us if we commend the gospel in that way. Jesus is, after all, not the soap powder that washes whiter. And we are not salespeople in his firm! Evangelism calls for much more sensitivity than that.

Equally, however, we need to speak with *confidence*. After all, we want to share not just one more opinion about religion, but the discovery we have made about Jesus of Nazareth. "I know whom I have believed," wrote Paul. We may not always know precisely *what* we have believed, but we know *whom*. That confidence needs to shine through what we say.

If that is the case, some *enthusiasm* may not be out of place! Many churchpeople seem to be remarkably unthrilled about their faith. Maybe that is because all they have is religion! But if you have discovered Jesus, the most wonderful and exciting person the world has ever seen, then you may be pardoned for displaying a touch of joy! I realize that ours is a cool, laid-back society. Enthusiasm is often suspect. But not when someone lands on the moon or scores a goal or wins a prize or gets engaged. Enthusiasm is in place then. And the enthusiasm of personal discovery should mark our conversation about Jesus. It has a real impact. I was talking on the phone to a television researcher yesterday, and she said, "You sound like such a happy man. . . . I've never heard anyone laugh like that on the phone." I told her that Jesus had made the difference, and she replied, "I do believe he must have."

But we must be *natural* in the way we talk about Jesus. Some Christians are so stilted and unnatural, it puts people off. Try to talk as naturally about him as you would about a human friend or some sporting event or an interesting discovery. Learn to move on and off the subject of Jesus with great ease, being happy to talk about him or to leave the topic, as seems natural under the circumstances and as your friends appear to want. After all, you want them to feel at ease. You get nowhere with them unless that is the case.

Another point to bear in mind as we talk to our friends about Christ is the *language* we use. Christians use all sorts of technical language, in-house stuff that is unintelligible to the average noninitiate. "Are you saved?" is not the most natural question to ask anyone, nor is it crystal clear what you mean! Language that has a lot of abstract nouns, most of them ending in *-ation,* is hardly likely to strike a light, either. The art of good communication is to put your message in the other person's language and to use illustrations familiar to the person you are talking to. So if you are talking to a carpenter, mention that your Boss is a carpenter, too, and that he wants to strip the rough edges and old varnish off us and use plane and chisel to create his vision in our lives. If you are speaking to a businessman, talk about the way Christ has underwritten our liabilities and wants to pump his resources into our lives and take us into partnership with him. We need to use imagination and empathy in the language we use. And on the whole we are very bad at it, so it is an area we need to work on.

The final point to bear in mind is *timing.* As in so many areas of life, timing is of the essence. The right thing at the wrong time can be a minor disaster. Keep very close to the Lord, and so sense from him whether now is the time to take matters further with a friend, or whether it would be better to say, "Why don't we have a talk about this tonight over coffee?" Timing is critical.

A FAVORABLE CLIMATE

If these are some of the things to bear in mind as we consider starting conversations about Jesus, then how do we create a favorable climate for such a conversation to take root?

One of the best ways is to *ask a question*—an unloaded one! This will enable you to see what is going on in your friend's mind and will also facilitate real give-and-take in the discussion rather than you pontificating about God! Some Christians make extensive use of a short questionnaire—that can be done even in the street. Most people do not mind answering if they are approached courteously and briefly; and it can lead to most useful results. But questions to your friend, such as, "Why do you think people feel so empty, even when they have so much?" or "Do you ever wonder if there is any overall purpose and meaning in our lives?" "Do you think faith in Jesus Christ spoils or enriches someone's life?" often open up a profitable conversation. One of the things we need to do if we are to help people to Christ is to puncture the apathy about ultimate issues, the cocoon of surface happiness with which our friends tend to protect themselves. Such questions often arouse self-questioning. That often leads to a genuine openness to consider an alternative viewpoint or way of life. There's your way in! You can provide that alternative viewpoint. It will withstand the most critical scrutiny.

One of the most effective evangelistic methods in America is based upon the use of questions. It originated with Dr. D. James Kennedy at Coral Ridge, Florida. It is called Evangelism Explosion. His way is to ask a couple of very simple but devastating questions, such as, "If you were to die tonight, would you be confident of going to heaven?" followed by "And why do you think God should let you into his heaven?" These are two superb diagnostic questions, especially for a culture where most people believe in heaven and want to go there. The questions are less effective, I think, in the European context, where fewer people seem to believe in heaven or care what happens to them when they die. But the point remains: get the right questions, and they open people up to consider the good news of Jesus seriously.

Another approach is to *point to some unusual mark of God's presence* and use it as a way in for the gospel. It might be the amazing compassion of Mother Teresa for people whom most would regard as terminal cases not worth bothering about. It might be a healing. Time and again I have found that a healing from cancer, or from a congenital inability to walk, in answer to prayer is a very potent approach to talking about Jesus with a friend. So is the transformation of someone known to you both, who has had a radical conversion. I think of an Oxford student when I was a rector in the city. This young woman was famous in her college for drunkenness and promiscuity. Then one summer she came face to face with Jesus Christ, and her life was turned right around. No more drunkenness. No more sleeping around. Inevitably, people were curious to know the reason for the change. It made a marvelous talking point, and she was responsible, directly or indirectly, for a good many people coming to trust Jesus for themselves during the following months.

Another very natural way of opening up a conversation is to *issue an invitation*. Why not ask that friend to something worthwhile: a lecture, a discussion, a church service, an outreach dinner, a sermon maybe? Choose the event carefully, or it may do more harm than good. But if you choose appropriately, the speaker can do more than half your work for you. And all you need to do to initiate the conversation afterward is to

ask, "What did you make of that?" I had a letter yesterday that illustrated this point well. My correspondent
wrote:

> On another matter, my wife and I were pleased to hear
> you at Spring Harvest in Minehead this year. A very
> good friend of mine, who has been fighting against
> Christianity for many years now, came along somewhat
> reluctantly with his wife and attended your session on
> the Resurrection. It was after this that he realized that
> he could have no intellectual objection to Christianity,
> and it was my privilege later in the week to pray with
> him as he made a commitment to Jesus Christ.

Notice the interlocking strands in that account. There
were the longstanding friendship, the holiday together,
the invitation to a challenging presentation, and the
personal conversation that followed and led to commitment. That scenario often happens, and it is easy to
initiate. We need only to build the bridges of friendship, wait for the appropriate occasion, invite the
friend, and then follow through with a conversation
flowing from the event.

Often we can open up a conversation when some
need becomes apparent. I shall never forget the day my
mother died. She was in a small side room off a ward of
older people who were, in effect, waiting for death. My
mother was desperately ill, and she, my father, and I
were hand in hand, praying. When we looked up, she
had gone. I do not know that I gave it much fore-
thought, but I went straight into the ward, told them
that my mother had died, and went on to tell them of
the hope of resurrection through Jesus in which my
mother believed and that was a door of hope to all of
them. The need was there all right. And the occasion
came to speak to it.

Or think of someone in bondage to alcohol or im-

mersed in witchcraft. The need is apparent. And it is
very easy and natural to speak about the power and the
vitality of the risen Lord Jesus, who is able to break the
fetters chaining us up. I think the challenge to us as
Christians is to confront these needs humbly but confi-
dently with some appropriate aspect of Jesus Christ as
we come across them. Loneliness, fear, meaninglessness—these are all common enough situations where
there is obvious need. We do not have any cause to be
shy about the remedy.

One of the easiest ways to get a meaningful conversation going is to sit down with a friend, *turn on the
TV,* and watch the news. It is almost bound to be so
full of pain and sheer human wickedness that it is a
simple matter to start a conversation on the basis of
what we have seen. "Why are human beings like this?"
"What is the fatal flaw in human nature that makes us
so awful to one another?" These questions are very
natural and get to the heart of the human problem very
speedily. From there it is a short step to Jesus.

There are times when a *play on words* gets a good
conversation going. The classic example of that in the
New Testament is when the Philippian jailer found his
jail in ruins after an earthquake and wondered how on
earth he was to face the civil authorities in the morning. "What must I do to be saved?" is what he is re-
ported to have said (Acts 16:30). It was no question
about his eternal destiny. It was all about how he was
going to get out of the mess he was in! Paul was on to
it in a flash: "I'll tell you how you can get out of the
mess you are in" was the thrust of what he said. "It has
to do with Jesus." If we listen sensitively—and at times
humorously—to the heart cries and unguarded comments of people around us, we can often find an entry
for the good news.

I recall once a man coming to stay because his car

had broken down. We booked time to talk after a particularly busy day. As soon as he came in he said, "I feel damned." I said to him, "That is precisely what you are!" I hasten to add that I do not normally behave in this way! But it was just the right approach for this existentialist in his alienation. I turned him to John 3:18: "Whoever does not believe stands *condemned already* because he has not believed in the name of God's one and only Son" (italics added). We began there. I showed him that God does not damn us for our sins and failures. But if we refuse his remedy for our situation, we stand self-condemned, and that was what he was experiencing in his life. He came to Christ with joy and gratitude that evening and began a remarkably wholehearted Christian life.

One of the very best ways of precipitating a serious discussion is to *tell your friend what Jesus has done for you.* Tell him your story in brief! This is becoming quite a common and respectable thing to do these days, and there is much to commend it. After all, "I have found" is a powerful thing. Nobody can deny what you have found, so it does not lead to argument or rejection. To have discovered something is in itself exciting and challenging. To say, "I have found," is an expression of fellowship, not an exhibition of preaching. If more Christians were prepared to bear humble and confident testimony to what they have found, it would be an enormous advantage to the Christian cause. It happens all the time in Asia and Africa, and that is one of the reasons why the gospel spreads so fast there. You are not a professional telling others what they must do, but very much an amateur, a friend, telling them what you have found and inviting them to try it for themselves. It is very attractive.

Yet talking your story is not enough by itself. It can sound egotistic. It can invite the response, "So you have found this? How nice for you." So as well as telling *your* story, you need to tell something of Jesus' story. And the wonderful thing is that his story is *history*. We date our era by it. It is rock solid. What God has done for your friends, as well as for you, is to come and die and rise again. So your discovery ("I have found") can become their discovery, too. It is in the light of these two stories, yours and his, that you invite your friends to make a response. We shall be looking more closely at that in subsequent chapters.

But I guess that the easiest of all ways to start a conversation about Christ that is likely to lead in a profitable direction is to *be so full of the Lord yourself* that you simply cannot help overflowing. Just as people in love cannot help themselves (it keeps bubbling out in words, looks, gestures), so the first Christians seemed to exude joy. And people wanted to know why. At Thessalonica, for example, the mixture of joy and confidence led to the rapid spread of the gospel (1Thess. 1:6). Their joy in Jesus enabled Paul and Silas to sing hymns of praise to God at midnight in a stinking Philippian jail when their backs were lacerated by whips and their feet were fast in the stocks (Acts 16:24–36). This inevitably flowed over into telling the jailer about Jesus the moment an opportunity presented itself. When people see that we have found treasure and are not ashamed to talk about it, questions will come thick and fast, and we find ourselves talking animatedly about the Lord before we know where we are.

Personal conversation is the best way of evangelism. It is natural. It can be done anywhere. It can be done by any Christian. It hits the mark. Let's avail ourselves of it.

4

Knowing the Good News

It is not much good gaining a friend's attention if we do not know what we are trying to communicate. What is the heart of the Christian good news? It is a massive subject, and its very size could easily awe us into feeling that it is all too difficult and there is no point in starting. But the gospel is like a sea—where an infant can safely paddle, but the tallest giraffe will be out of its depth. So let us take heart, and look at the following seven propositions. They do not exhaust the Christian good news, but they lie very near the heart of it and will provide at least a starting point for discussion with a friend. And make no mistake, there will be discussion because each of these seven points flies in the face of much that is believed in secular society.

1. GOD

Recently, the bishop of Chichester in England fired a pastor who did not believe in God. Hardly politically correct, maybe, but the bishop was quite right. Christians believe in the existence of God—a power so great that it brought the whole world into existence, and yet so intimate that it is revealed in the tiniest details of our world. We believe in the God of the universe, the God of the atom. Moreover, we believe that this God is personal. Part of his creation is humankind, created, we believe, in his image, and we are personal; so though he may be beyond personality, God must be at least personal. This God is concerned with right and wrong, and has built a conscience into us to be a moral direction finder. What is more, God formed us to know him and enjoy him forever, for he is not only power and intelligence, but love. He was not prepared to leave us in our ignorance: instead, he set about revealing himself to us. He did it through the created world. He did it through history, particularly the history of the Jewish people. He did it through prophets, much of whose work is contained in the Bible. And supremely, he did it through Jesus, in whom he disclosed himself to us as fully as we can comprehend. He is the originating cause of the universe. He is its goal and destiny. He is the principle of coherence within it. Our God is that big. He is worthy of worship.

Now you can't expect your friend to take that in without discussion. He may believe it already, in which case you can move on without debate. But he may think of God as the impersonal ground of being or as nature or whatever. There are some very weird ideas about God around these days. So are there any good reasons why we Christians believe as we do? There are indeed. They are solid facts. Here they are in a nutshell:

The fact of the world. What accounts for life on this earth? If it is all a matter of chance, how come that cause and effect operate everywhere? How come the laws of nature?

The fact of design. There is abundant evidence of intelligent design in our world. It is even more apparent in nature than in the artifacts intelligent human beings design. Why? Because "the heavens are telling the glory of God; and the firmament proclaims his handiwork" (Ps. 19:1 NRSV).

The fact of personality. A live person is utterly different from a corpse or a robot. Can the personal spring from the impersonal? Can the higher (human personality) be derived form the lower (brute matter, devoid of a Creator)? Does that make sense?

The fact of values. We all have them, however we explain it. Beauty, truth, goodness, creativity, humor, love, goodness—did they spring from time, chance, and impersonal matter? Yet that is all you are left with if there is no Creator.

The fact of conscience. We all have one, however much we argue against it and try to muzzle it. It is not an infallible guide, but it points to standards that we "ought" (i.e., "owe it"—but to what or whom?) to keep. It cannot be explained as social conditioning, for it often points away from what is to what should be. This inner law strongly suggests the existence of a moral Lawgiver who put it there. No other explanation has proved convincing.

The fact of religion. Man is a religious animal. He must worship God or create his own idol, and this has been the case worldwide and throughout human history—without exception. Is the universal religious instinct the only one of our instincts that has no reality to satisfy it? If so, how do you account for its prevalence and power? Sleep satisfies our instinct for rest, food our instinct for hunger, intercourse our instinct for sex. What satisfies our instinct for God? Is not Augustine right in saying, "O God, you have made us for yourself, and our hearts are restless until they find their rest in you"?

The fact of Jesus. More of this later on; but an intelligent Creator, personal, moral, the source of values, concerned for our worship and companionship, remains an unknown God unless he chooses to reveal himself. This he has done in Jesus. And Jesus is the strongest of all arguments for the reality of God.

2. CREATION

This is a particularly important topic these days, with the Green movement and widespread ecological concern. Christians have good reason to be ashamed because we have not been in the forefront of the move to save the world from the ravages of twentieth-century spoliation. Human beings poison the seas, create deserts, cut down the forests, cause the greenhouse effect, smash the ozone layer—all in the name of capitalism and progress—and there has been hardly a squeak out of the church. But there should have been, for we have the best of all reasons for caring about this earth.

We believe the world is not random, but created by the good God who has left us, as the crown of his creation, to tend it. We are meant to be *over* the creation but *under* God. Instead, we have certainly shown our mastery over creation, but we are not masters of ourselves. Instead of holding the world in trust for God, we have spit in his eye and argued that he does not exist. So our record is unimpressive, but our account of the world is convincing. We see it as neither divine (like the New Agers and the Hindus) nor expendable (like the materialists). We do not worship it; we do not rape it. We know we are accountable for our handling of it, and we do not make exploitation of natural resources a god. It is God's world, not ours, and we are his stewards—no more and no less. That is a noble view of humankind and creation, and we can hold our heads high in any Green debate. Modern young people, in particular, resonate with this aspect of Christian belief. But we need to have proper humility as we confess how far our actions have fallen short of our convictions.

A Christian understanding of the natural world means we need never give way to the despair of the doom-watch brigade. We are well aware of the wickedness of human nature and have little faith in man to save the planet. But we believe in God the Creator, Sustainer, and Renewer of the universe. Indeed, we look to a new heaven and a new earth. Although we would be hard put to explain precisely what we mean by that, we know we are on the right track because of the remarkable natural properties of the soil, vegetation, and marine and human life to regenerate after all manner of disasters. The God who instilled that principle into our world can be trusted not to allow it finally to destroy itself.

3. HUMANKIND

Here again, the Christian view is distinctive. We do not see human beings as naked apes or as little angels. We see them as made in God's image and designed to share life in company with him. When God looked at man and his environment at the dawn of history, he declared all of it very good. But you have only to turn over one more page at the very beginning of the Bible story to see that it did not stay that way. Man used his God-given free will to turn his back on God, to break his laws, and to spurn his company. The result is that we have become a mixture of good and bad. The divine image has not been completely destroyed in us, but it has been badly damaged, sometimes beyond recognition. The good news is that it can be restored, once Christ is given a chance in our lives.

The longer I live, the more confident I am in the biblical assessment of humankind. It refuses to side with the optimistic humanists and pretend that all is well with us—that view has nothing to commend it after the atrocities of two world wars, or Rwanda and Bosnia; it is only held nowadays in the ivory towers of some university seminar rooms. But neither does the Bible accept the dismal analysis of human nature offered by the pessimistic humanists, particularly the existentialists, who see man as a crumpled piece of paper in the rain. No, there is more to humankind than that. The Christian view seems to me to be the genuinely realistic one, which sees us as a temple, but a temple in ruins. It sees us as a lovely garden, but a garden that has run wild and is full of weeds. The temple can be restored. The garden can be recultivated. But only when the Owner is invited to take charge.

There is, therefore, something tremendously hopeful about the Bible's understanding of our race. We are fallen, it is true. That Fall has affected every part of us —our appetites, our conscience, our intellect, our relationship with God and with each other. But the last Adam reversed the implications of the Fall. In him the image of God can be restored in any one of us. Humankind is not junk; man is not beyond redemption.

Individual transformation is possible. So is the formation of God's counterculture, made up of men and women who have made room for their rightful Lord and are living out their lives in allegiance to him. That is the true, biblical realism about the human condition that should commend itself to many a thoughtful inquirer.

4. JESUS

Jesus is the centerpiece of God's revelation of himself, just as he is the centerpiece of God's rescue of humankind. It is critical, therefore, that we are clear about who he is. Then we can look at what he has done.

Who Is This Jesus?

Well, he was a human being, like us. He was hungry like us, exhausted like us, joyful like us, disappointed like us. He suffered and bled like us. He died, just as we have to. He was truly one of us. And yet that is not the whole story. All the New Testament writers, and millions since all over the world, have been convinced that he is more than just a man. He is no less than God, come to our rescue.

So much rubbish about Jesus is constantly on sale in books and on film that you may well need to establish the existence of Jesus from secular sources, such as Tacitus's *Annals* 15.44; Josephus's *Antiquities* 18.3; Pliny's *Epistles* 10.96; and Suetonius's *Claudius* 25. You may care to loan friends a copy of my *Who Is This Jesus?* or F. F. Bruce's *The Real Jesus,* both of which conveniently summarize and quote the non-Christian evidence for Jesus. That he existed and was crucified, and his tomb was empty three days later—all that is incontrovertible. But was he more than man? That is the crux.

Remember that the Jews, the original people among whom he lived, were the most passionate monotheists. They were the hardest people in the world to convince that he was more than man. Yet many became convinced by several factors:

His character. It has dominated humankind from that day to this, appealing equally to men and women, young and old, all types and nationalities. His balance, his qualities, his attractiveness, his love, especially for the unlovely—all this has persuaded thoughtful people that he was more than man. What was there in his heredity and environment that explains such a character, who combines all the characteristic virtues of men and women—with none of the vices?

His teaching. It is the most wonderful teaching the world has ever known. Nothing like it has ever emerged, before or since. Its authority, its pungency, its profundity, and its clarity set it apart from all other teaching. You only have to read it to be convinced. Take your friend to the Sermon on the Mount and expose him to some of it, especially its conclusion.

His behavior. He taught the highest standards, and unlike any other human being before or since, he kept them. Buddha did not manage that, good though his life was. Nor did Muhammad. Nor did Socrates. They did not even claim to. Jesus' life was a moral miracle. He claimed to be without sin. Every strand of the New Testament shows that his followers, who knew him intimately, agreed. Even his enemies, Judas, Pilate, and the Pharisees, could not uphold a contradictory claim.

His miracles. We need never be embarrassed about the miracles of Jesus. They are embedded in almost all strands of the tradition about Jesus, reaching back as it does to within a few years of his death. There is Jewish attestation to them as well. They were never done for selfish ends. They were never done to show off. They are pointers to who he is. They do not prove his deity (nothing could do that), but they are highly congruent with it. If God really came into our world, you would expect things to be a little different! And the most important and significant of his miracles concern the beginning and end of his life—his incarnation and resurrection. These are the really mind-blowing things that attest his claim like nothing else.

His fulfillment of prophecy. Different strands of the Old Testament's predictions were fulfilled in him: Son of man; Son of God; Son of David; Suffering Servant; Melchizedek; the ultimate prophet, priest, and king; one greater than the temple; one greater than Moses; one greater than Solomon; and so on. He is even portrayed as the replacer of the Law and the embodiment of the shekinah, the glory of God. Such a claim to fulfillment, all concentrated in a single individual, is without parallel in world literature. Many prophecies concerned his birth and death, the two areas of life where it is hardest to fake fulfillment!

His claims. He claimed God as his *Abba* (an utterly unique filial relationship). He claimed to forgive sins, to merit worship, to rise from death, to judge humankind, to be the way to God, to be the truth about God, and to embody the very life of God himself. What are we to make of claims like these? Are they the ravings of a madman? The cruel deceit of a crook? Or taken with all the other indicators, do they not have about them the ring of truth?

His death. The unselfishness of it, the sacrifice of it, the sin-bearing of it, the victory of it, drew all sorts of people to him, and still do. The fact that such a person went willingly to such a fate, and the interpretation he gave of it, convinced them. The Resurrection made them certain.

His resurrection. We need to give special attention to the Resurrection because it is central to the Christian claim. Without it there is no clinching evidence that Jesus was more than a great teacher. If it is true, it sets Jesus apart once and for all as the unique Son of God (Rom. 1:4). Nobody else rose from the dead to a new dimension of endless life. But did he? You may find these points helpful as you talk this vital matter over with your friend; five factors point in the same direction;

Jesus was dead. The public execution, the centurion's death certificate given to the governor, the blood and water (i.e., clot and serum in separation—strong medical proof of death), Pilate's ceding the corpse to Jesus' followers after the execution, all show that no Passover plot (arguing that Jesus was not quite dead but revived) will do as an explanation. Jesus was dead all right. The Romans were experts at the grisly task of crucifixion. Their victims did not survive.

The tomb was empty. That is agreed all around. It was empty because of divine or human intervention. If the latter, then it must have been the friends or the enemies of Jesus who did it. But his friends could not: they were psychologically incapable of it, and in any case they would have been unable to get past the stone and the guard on the tomb. However, the enemies of Jesus would certainly not remove his body: they were only too delighted to have him dead at last and would have done nothing to disturb the situation. Even if they had, they could easily have pointed to the new grave when the disciples started setting Jerusalem alight with their preaching of Jesus' resurrection. No, there is no credible alternative to the unanimous Christian claim that God raised Jesus from the dead. And that makes sense of the empty tomb, the state of the grave clothes, the flight of the guard, and the dawning of Easter faith.

The church was born. The followers of Jesus initially had nothing to distinguish them from orthodox Jews, apart from their convictions about Jesus and the Resurrection. Their three major innovations—baptism, the Eucharist, and Sunday observance—are all incomprehensible without the Resurrection. The worldwide movement that we know as Christianity was launched by the Resurrection.

Jesus appeared. Over a period of six weeks Jesus appeared to a wide cross-section of people: the Eleven, James, Peter, Thomas, the five hundred, Mary Magdalene, the Virgin Mary, and others. No hallucination theory will bear serious investigation. The Resurrection appearances have no parallel anywhere in the world's history. They are unique, just as Jesus was unique.

Lives were changed. The lives of the people who met Jesus after the Resurrection were transformed. The mercurial Peter became a man of rock. Paul, the persecutor, became a convinced apostle. James, the skeptical brother of Jesus, became leader of the Jerusalem church. The rabble who had deserted him and fled became the dynamic church we read about in the Acts. No prison, no death sentence, could stop them from proclaiming to all and sundry that Jesus is alive and can be met. Lives were changed then, and they have been changed ever since. The glory of Christianity is the way Jesus takes sinners on board and makes them saints by the power of his Resurrection life at work in them. This is real. No Resurrection myth theory will hold water.

All these strands point in the same direction; their impact is cumulative. And the assurance that Jesus is risen and alive has not grown more speculative and remote, but has deepened and spread worldwide in the succeeding centuries. Nowadays more than a third of humankind subscribe to it. It is the final attestation to who Jesus is.

5. RESCUE

We are now in a position to understand what Jesus offers to us. It is of the utmost importance that you get the essence of this across to your friend. But first of all you have to show him who Jesus really is, or he will never understand the glory of what Jesus offers.

You see, it is God almighty who came to this earth in order to find the likes of us. It is God almighty who went to that terrible cross for us. It is God almighty whom the grave could not hold, but who rose to newness of life. That's who we are talking about. No great teacher. No impressive guru. But God.

WHY DID HE COME?

He came to show us what God is really like. And because we could never understand the infinite God, he humbled himself and became one of us—to show us, in the form of a human being, what he is like. "Anyone who has seen me has seen the Father" was his claim (John 14:9). He is the human face of God. And so we need never plead ignorance of God. We know all that we can understand, for he has shown it to us in the life and death of Jesus. His compassion, his care, his truthfulness, his purity, his sacrifice—it is all there, fleshed out in Jesus of Nazareth.

He went further than this. He died to take responsibility for the evil in all of our lives. It is obvious enough that a holy God cannot condone human wickedness. And we cannot escape a share in that wickedness: it is the same human disease. That is apparent in some current secular admissions that came my way only today. Dave Stewart, a major musician, was asked, "When you look in the mirror, do you like what you see?" His answer was short and to the point: "No." God doesn't like it, either. Karl Lagerfeld of Chanel, one of the foremost designers in the world, admits his self-loathing as he sees the models going down the catwalk: "I hate it. You feel dirty. There are all those creatures up there and you are like a worn out piece of garbage." Kurt Cobain, lead singer of Nirvana and hero of the younger generation, committed suicide in 1994 because he could not live with himself anymore: "I'm a stain. I'm so ugly . . . I hate myself and I want to die."

Yes, there is a stain in all our lives, a dark stain. We are ugly, compared with the unutterable beauty of God. And God cannot pretend that this is not the case. So God did the unimaginable. He took the evil in us upon himself. He underwent the doom of death our sins deserved. He took our place so that we could quite justly be forgiven and taken back into God's presence —for free! What incredible generosity! What wonderful news! God almighty holds nothing against us. The accusing load of our misdoings has been nailed to the cross of Jesus, and he has gladly taken the rap for them. If that is not good news, I don't know what is. I have seen it transform the lives of people who had given up hope—in all five continents and in quite a few prisons, too.

He came. He died. And he rose. That is the third really vital thing to get across. Because Jesus really did rise from the dead, he is alive, and we can meet him. A Christian is someone who has, in fact, made contact with the living Jesus. Real Christianity is not so much a religion as a relationship—with Jesus. Yes, because he is alive, I can meet him. Because he is alive, he can be my constant companion. Because he is alive, the power that raised him from the tomb is able to raise me from the downward pull of the evil tendencies and bad habits in my life. There is a lot of truth and good theology in the simple children's chorus written many years ago:

Jesus died to set me free from the guilt of sin.
Jesus lives that I may be strong the fight to win.

That is our Jesus. That is what he has achieved for us.
Alleluia!

6. COMMUNITY

One of the diseases in the Western world is individualism. It has strengths: anyone in the U.S. or Canada will
tell you that rugged individualism won the West. But it
has terrible weaknesses, too. It fosters the illusion that
we can live a complete life without one another. The
Christian gospel rejects that notion out of hand. People
may come to Jesus on their own, one by one (though
sometimes it happens with whole communities at a
time), but they never stay like that. God is not primarily concerned with saving individuals. He is concerned
with forming a new community. He wants to put a
Society of Jesus in place, a Community of the Resurrection, a counterculture. He does not merely want us to
talk about reconciliation, love, and trust, but to live
them out. In this sense, the church itself is part of the
good news. For Christianity is inescapably communal.
The church is not an optional extra for those who like
that kind of thing. It is an integral part of the kingdom
of God.

It is not the kingdom (God forbid!). But it is the part
of God's kingdom that is glad to acknowledge him
King, that tries to serve and please him, and to extend
to his rebel subjects God's invitation to lay down their
arms and welcome his rule. That understanding at
once gives us three important characteristics of the
church: it is *corporate,* comprising people of all back-
grounds and colors who acknowledge Jesus as King; it
is meant to be *holy,* demonstrating a different style of

life from that in the world still in rebellion against God; and it has a job to do—*mission.*

All Christians are part of this divine society. We can't help it. The Christianity that does not begin with the individual does not begin. But the Christianity that ends with the individual ends. That is why Jesus set about building a community of disciples while he was on earth. That is why he inaugurated a joining ceremony, baptism, that was so clearly initiation into a community. That is why he left behind him not a rule book but a meal—the very essence of partnership and belonging.

A clear understanding of the place of the church in the purpose of God is essential. Otherwise, it is so easy to give up on the church. It is full of sin—because it is full of sinners like you and me! But God has not given up on the church. He cherishes it like his bride. He wants to show *through the church* to the principalities and powers of darkness what he can do with a community of people who, however weak and sinful, entrust their lives to him (Eph. 3:10). And so we must be clear that in introducing a friend to Jesus, we are also introducing that friend to the community of Jesus. It is as stupid to try to be a Christian without the church as to be a child without the family. God takes us in our soiled and solitary state, cleans us up, and puts us in his family. That is an aspect of the good news we must never forget to mention.

7. DESTINY

In the last century, Christians may have concentrated too much on the final destiny of human beings. Heaven and hell perhaps figured too large in Christian teaching. But undeniably, the pendulum has swung the other way, and nowadays we do not think about our final destiny nearly enough. We see this life not as preparation for the life to come, but as our more or less permanent abode; and when a friend has to leave it, this is most regrettable and we mention it only in muffled whispers. There is a notable unwillingness to talk about death today. It is the forbidden subject.

Yet, once again, the Christian gospel challenges current political correctness. We Christians need have no fear of death; it is a defeated foe. Jesus broke its back when he rose from the dead. Part of his triumph was "through death to destroy him who had the power of death, that is the devil, and deliver all those who through fear of death were subject to lifelong bondage" (Heb. 2:14–15, author's translation). To be sure, none of us looks forward to the process of dying, but we need have no dread of being dead! For to die is to "depart and be with Christ, which is better by far" (Phil. 1:23). It is something to look forward to. We shall forever be with the Lord, and that is the utter fulfillment of all our wildest hopes.

Sometimes you hear people say, "I was saved on such and such a day." Well, that is a partial truth. Sometimes *saved* is used in the past tense in the Bible, but very rarely. Salvation has three tenses in Scripture: I *have been saved* from the *guilt* of sin through Christ's death on the cross; I *am being saved* from the *power* of sin (or not, as the case may be!) through his risen life in me; and I *will be saved* from the *presence* of sin when I go to join him in his heavenly home. Heaven, you see, is not some happy ending tacked on to the story of God's rescue in this life. It is an integral part of all he plans to do for his children. He burdens himself with our badness. He puts his Spirit into our lives. He gradually changes us individually and molds us into a community that shows something of his harmony, variety, unity, love, and service. And at the end of the day he welcomes us to his home in heaven. Fittingly, then, the last chapters of the Bible are all about that heavenly home and our relationship with one another and with him in unimaginable joy forever.

Isn't it a wonderful thought that God has determined not to scrap humanity, as well he might? He has planned for us the most glorious future. And the proof that this is no mere pie in the sky is the Resurrection. It is the certain pledge of God's future. Jesus is currently the only resurrection body in existence. But we shall share his nature one day in the new heaven and new earth. It is the destiny he has for us, and it is all sheer grace, undeserved love. No wonder Christians are full of praise and gratitude when they are being true to their nature!

I do not for a moment suggest that you will need to go through all seven of these points with your friend if you are going to lead him or her to Christ. But you may well find it helpful to have them as pegs, so to speak, on which you can hang some of the things you want to say. They may come in handy as a sort of minitheology, from which you will draw as you need. Some people will particularly need the emphasis on creation or final destiny. Some will see the glory and the shame of human nature in clear colors for the first time. Some will come to recognize that God is real, or that the Resurrection genuinely happened. But all will need to know how far we have strayed from God, and the immensity of the rescue plan he launched at tremendous cost. That is the heart of the good news, and when once a man really comes to understand that, it makes a new person of him. It's the start of a new life. "Therefore, if anyone is in Christ, he is a new creation; the old has gone, the new has come!" (2 Cor. 5:17).

5

Becoming the Midwife

I hope the time will come in conversation with your friend when you can actually help him to cross over into a thoughtful commitment to Jesus Christ. You will, perhaps, be given the immense privilege of becoming the midwife at the birth.

That is actually a good analogy. The midwife does not produce the birth; she merely helps it along. And no Christian converts another. At best we help the process along—a process that is the fruit of God's message lodging in the heart, like a seed in the womb. It is always God who gives the new life, but he sometimes allows us to be present at its birth and even to assist.

There is another thing about the midwife. I suppose she could make either of two mistakes. One would be to treat every birth the same way and approach each situation with cold professionalism. No young mother would appreciate that; and the midwife herself would miss individual needs and be blinded to the wonder of it all. What is more, that path would be disastrous if there were any complications in the birth—and complications usually arise bringing spiritual new life to birth! The other mistake would be for the midwife to have not the slightest clue what to do. Mercifully, that rarely happens in that profession, but it happens all too often in Christian circles. If someone asks us how to begin Christian discipleship, it simply will not do to waffle. We need to be able to give quiet but confident directions, as a midwife would to the young mother.

What is needed, then, is a clear idea of how to help someone to Christ, coupled with a lot of flexibility in our approach. We must not offer people a hardline program; but neither must we be like the fisherman who, on his return home empty-handed, was asked by his wife, "How many did you catch?" He had to reply sadly, "None actually, but I influenced a good many."

What follows must not, therefore, be taken for a technique. You are not a manipulator, but an introducer. You have reached a point in the conversation when your friend genuinely wants to start a relationship with Christ. How can you help him to begin?

I generally have the first four letters of the alphabet in the back of my mind at this point. However flexibly I approach it, however often I am diverted by his questions or concerns, four things seem important if he is to come to know Christ. First, there is something to *admit*—that he is not in living touch with God and needs to get right with him. Second, there is something to *believe*—that God in Christ has done everything needed for our restoration. Third, there is something to *consider*—the cost of discipleship. Fourth, there is something to *do*—to reach out in faith and personally appropriate the proffered gift.

There are many alternative ways of presenting these truths. The most basic is the one we find in the New Testament itself: *repent, believe,* and *be baptized. Repent* of the alienation from God we have lived in for so long, the guilt and power of the evil that is interwoven with our lives. *Believe* in the God who made the world and yet cares so much for us that he entered his own world as a human being, died to deal with our alienation and guilt, and lives to change us from the inside. And *be baptized* because baptism is the mark both of what God has done for us and of our commitment to Christ. It means initiation into Christ and into his church. This pattern should be easiest of all for us to use, but in practice it has gotten complicated: some Christians baptize infants, while others baptize only those able to make a personal response. And many people were baptized in infancy who have no Christian faith whatever, let alone personal discipleship.

Consequently, other outlines seem called for. Many are in use. One of the most common is the "step program"—steps to peace with God. First, *God's purpose*—peace and life for all his people; second, *our problem*—separation from that loving God; third, *God's remedy*—the cross of Christ; and fourth, *our response*—to receive the Holy Spirit of Jesus into our lives.

Some people like to explain it diagrammatically. You can do that with a single verse of Scripture, which you expand on appropriately. (See Figure 1.) Romans 6:23 is a good example, but you could find your own preferred verse of Scripture. This one shows the contrast in two alternative ways of living. You are either in the country that culminates in death or else in the one that leads to life. You are either following God or else following the self-centered principle that Christians call sin. And you are either relying on something you do to get you home safe and dry at the end of the day or else relying on a free gift. That is a massive contrast. We are all in one category or the other. Mercifully, it is possible to move from one situation into the other "through Jesus Christ our Lord."

Another diagram that many people have found helpful is very simple and can be drawn on a piece of paper in the home or a paper napkin in a restaurant. (See figure 2.) The first picture shows God's plan for the

For the *wages* of *sin* is *death*,
but the *gift* of *God* is *eternal life*
through *Jesus Christ* our *Lord*.
—Romans 6:23

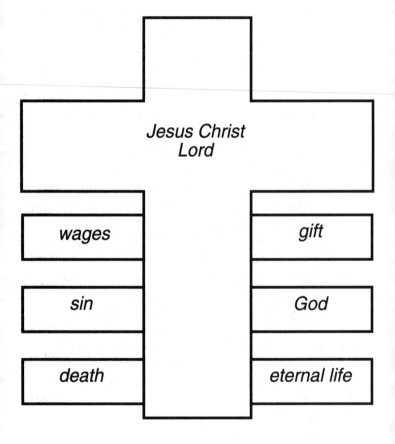

Figure 1

world, with humankind as his steward and intermediary. The second shows man's refusal to live in allegiance to God and his rejection of God's authority. The third shows that God cannot tolerate this rebellion and has to judge us. Then comes part two of the drawing. The fourth picture shows Jesus as the Proper Man, succeeding where we have failed; he is shown cruciform, to demonstrate that God's way of putting us right with him comes through the cross of Christ. The fifth picture shows the risen Jesus ascended to his home in heaven, alive and sharing the reign of God. And the final picture faces us with a choice. Are we going to crown Jesus as sovereign in our lives or to persist in wearing the crown ourselves? The verse of Scripture, John 3:36, is particularly challenging.

These are some of the ways people like to explain the good news to their friends. I have nothing but admiration for having a clear outline up your sleeve, so long as you realize that it is only a very truncated presentation of the gospel and you must never suggest that it is the whole story or the only way to help someone to Christ. Remember that different needs in the people you talk to will make different aspects of Jesus attractive. Remember, too, that God can work very effectively without any human intermediaries like you and me. God loves to use us, but he can manage on his own!

Here is an example of what I mean. This conversion was entirely the work of God through a liturgical church service:

> During my time at University I tried to fill the gap in my life which I can only surmise was due to the absence of God. I tried drink, drugs, sex, in fact anything that was offered, all to no avail. Eventually I met a dedicated Christian: she tried to evangelize me, and I tried to break her.

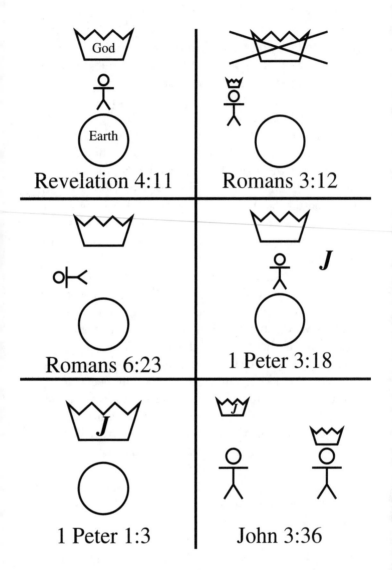

Figure 2

I recall waking one Sunday morning after a particularly heavy party and thinking "I must go to church," and actually acting on the impulse. I wound up at the local Anglo-Catholic church and went to the service.

During that hour, I met with God in what can only be described as the quietest and most powerful moment of my life. In the liturgy I met with a God who was alive and in the world—totally unlike any kind of God I had known before. And in the Communion I met the God who had died to save me, and loved me a way that only God could.

This was my time of becoming a Christian, and meeting with the God I will serve until the end of the age.

That was indeed the beginning of Mark's discipleship. It continues. He is now training for ordination! And it shows us very clearly that the work of the new birth is God's work, not ours.

Nevertheless, God does allow us to help. And that is why I want to return to the situation outlined at the beginning of this chapter, where you are confronted by someone who genuinely wants to know the way to get started. I also want to expand on the "first four letters of the alphabet" approach to which I referred, and which I find particularly helpful.

A. THERE IS SOMETHING TO ADMIT

Gently but firmly show your friend that at the heart of all the confusions and failures in his life—his emptiness, lack of meaning, or whatever the presenting problem may be—is the fact that he has left God out of account. He has gone his own way. He is facing the pain of living without God in a world where the only lasting joy is to live in company with God. In a word,

he has the human disease of sin. It consists of breaking
God's laws for human life and happiness (1 John 3:4),
coming short of his standards (James 4:17), and rejecting his love and authority over us (John 3:18). The
results of this human disease are very serious. We find
ourselves estranged from God (Isa. 59:1–2; Eph. 2:1)
and enslaved to our self-centeredness (John 8:34; Titus
3:3; 2 Peter 2:19). The disease is fatal if it is not dealt
with (Rom. 6:23).

If people are going to begin a living relationship
with Christ, they need to accept the Bible's diagnosis of
the basic problems in their lives. They need to see that
they are in the wrong with God. They need to be willing to change.

At this point you will hit your biggest problem—
human pride. We are most reluctant to admit that we
are in the wrong on anything, let alone the direction of
our whole lives. We will struggle to prove that it can't
be as bad as that. But the Bible, with its ruthless realism, will not let us off the hook. It maintains that so far
from having, as we fondly imagine, a heart of gold, "the
human heart is deceitful above all things and desperately wicked" (Jer. 17:9, author's translation). Instead
of evil being something outside us, associated with
training, background, and circumstances, evil has its
root within us, for "it is from within, from the human
heart, that evil intentions come: fornication, theft,
murder, adultery, avarice, wickedness, deceit, licen-
tiousness, envy, slander, pride, folly. All these evil
things come from within, and they defile a person"
(Mark 7:21–23 NRSV). That was Jesus speaking. Would
you care to argue that he was wrong in his analysis? He
was not wrong. Every newscast and every morning's
newspaper underline it. Our human nature is defiled.
It is dirty. It needs cleaning up.

Of course, people have recognized this down the
ages and have devised all kinds of ways to handle the

situation. Some argue that evil is unreal—until one of their own relations is gunned down by a bandit or their daughter assaulted. Some say that they have never done any wrong—just ask their relatives or employers! "If we claim to be without sin, we deceive ourselves and the truth is not in us" (1 John 1:8). We certainly don't deceive anyone else. Some people imagine that God will put their good deeds in one side of his scale and their bad deeds in the other and, being a God of mercy, he will probably let them scrape through. Not so. He will put Jesus (who embodied what God expects of human nature at its best) in one side of the scale and us, with all our mix of good and bad, in the other. We shall all weigh light. None of us will be fit to be seen. Some people will deny that evil has any grip on their lives, but they will give the game away immediately; you will discover that they are enslaved to tobacco, coffee, slandering other people, drugs, pornography, or something. Everyone is a slave who has not been liberated by Jesus. There are no exceptions. Even if your friend could live an absolutely spotless life from now until the end of his life, what about the past? The guilty stains from the past would be unchanged. The skeletons from the past would still be in the cupboard. As the letter to the Romans laconically observes, "There is no one righteous, not even one" (3:10). And God, who is by definition pure and holy and just, cannot overlook all this. He cannot have defilement in his holy presence. It stands to reason.

B. THERE IS SOMETHING TO BELIEVE

Mercifully, we do not have to believe a lot to become a Christian. The content of our faith will grow in the months and years that follow. The earliest Christian confession was simply "Jesus is Lord." That says it all, really. *Jesus* means "God to the rescue." And *Lord* is an exalted name, often used in the Bible for God. So what that short confession means is something like this: "God himself has come to our rescue. And he is risen and exalted as Lord of the universe, of the church, and of me personally." That is God's answer to our problem. He became incarnate for us, died for us, is alive for us, and calls for our allegiance.

You will need to take time to show your friend how wonderfully God has met our need, how brilliantly he has devised a cure for the human disease. Through his death on the cross, Jesus dealt with our guilt by taking it upon himself (Rom. 5:1; 8:1; 2 Cor. 5:21; 1 Peter 3:18). Because of his resurrection, he is alive and can be met. He can be our companion in this life and our sure guide to the life to come. After all, nobody else has risen from the dead!

You will need to help your friend understand something of the cross of Jesus. Few people grasp it easily—which is not surprising, since it is the ultimate mystery. But the Cross is certainly not just the demonstration of God's love. It is certainly not a good man coming to a difficult end. It is certainly not a martyr stoically enduring his fate. No. It is God himself dealing with our sins by taking the weight of them on his own shoulders. Verses from the Bible like Mark 10:45; 2 Corinthians 5:18, 21; and Galatians 3:10, 13 give shafts of light on different aspects of the central mystery. I find it almost incredible that God should love a person like me enough to come and rescue me by enduring the most horrible death that could ever be designed by the brutality of man. More still, that he should allow the world's evil—and in particular my evil—to be poured out in vile concentration on his sinless head. But he did. And that is why it is Good Friday for us, Bad Friday though it was for him. That is why we can cry out with confident exultation, "There is now no condemnation for those who are in Christ Jesus" (Rom. 8:1).

But one of the verses that I find most helpful in explaining to inquirers what Jesus did for them on the cross is 1 Peter 3:18: "Christ has once suffered for sins, the just for the unjust, to bring us to God" (author's translation). Simple and clear. The sufferer on the cross was none other than the Christ, the anointed deliverer, for whom the world had been waiting since the Garden of Eden. It was the Supreme Rescuer who ended up in naked agony on that terrible tree. Why was he there? "For sins": he, "the just," took the place that should rightly have fallen to us, "the unjust," if we really got our deserts from a holy God. After all, it had always been the case that the wages of sin was death. We already experience the emotional, social, and spiritual aspects of that death in our state of self-selected alienation. Physical death merely completes the final separation. So that is why his death was needed. "To bring us to God": had there been any other way, we can be sure he would have taken it. But there was no other way. There on the cross he did all that was necessary to bring us back to the God we so earnestly keep away from. And it happened "once"; the Greek word used here means not "once upon a time" but "once and for all." The job has been done. The ransom price has been paid.

And just as Christ's death cleans up the record of our accusing past, so the resurrection of Jesus can release in our lives a power that makes for radical change. The Risen One offers to come and take up residence in our lives, so as to release in us the power of his resurrection (Eph. 1:19; Phil. 4:13; 1 Peter 1:5). He will progressively break down the bondage to self-will that spoils us and set us free to be and to behave as sons and daughters in his family (John 8:36). That is what you are encouraging your friend to believe. Not many things, but things of vast significance. Not a creed, but the person of the living God who came and died and rose. And it is not a fairy story, but firmly anchored in history. It is eminently worthy of belief.

C. THERE IS SOMETHING TO CONSIDER

That is, what it will cost to be a disciple of Jesus. The entrance to the Christian life is free, but the annual subscription is everything we have. Jesus is not merely Savior. He is Lord. And you will save yourself and your friend a lot of trouble later on if you make it very plain at the outset that it will be a costly thing to follow Christ. Jesus laid it on the line very clearly in Luke 14:25–35, immediately after emphasizing in the parable of the great supper that the kingdom is gloriously free for all comers. He asked the crowds to consider whether they were prepared to face obedience to him even before family and personal wishes. Were they ready for a lifetime of commitment? Were they willing to be opposed? Could they cope with being in a minority? Dare they be salt to society? Such were some of the elements in the costly discipleship to which Jesus called people. They have not changed!

Of course, all this lies in the future. You cannot expect your friend at the moment of commitment to have any realistic idea of what it will cost him, any more than the bridal couple can have any idea on their wedding day of what it will cost them twenty years down the road to be pledged to each other for better, for worse, for richer, for poorer. But there needs to be that willingness in principle to put each other first, come wind, come weather. It is like that with commitment to Jesus. He put it very sharply in Matthew 6:24: "You cannot serve both God and Mammon" (the Carthaginian god of wealth). It is costly to be a Christian, and we must never disguise that fact. But we need to make plain to a friend that it is also extremely costly to reject Jesus and his offer of eternal life, pardon, and fulfillment.

I often summarize this aspect of becoming a Christian by posing three questions. Are you willing to let Christ clean up the wrong things in your life, many of which will have become old friends by now? Are you willing to put Jesus in the number one slot? And are you willing to be known as a Christian and join the Christian community? That is about as far as he will be able to see, for the present. But you owe it to him to put this matter of the cost of discipleship fairly and squarely before him.

D. THERE IS SOMETHING TO DO

Your friend needs to receive the gift, which is Jesus himself. All God's other gifts are wrapped up in him (Eph. 1:3). There are many pictures in the New Testament of the way in which we, in our weakness, and Christ, in his love and power, get together. We believe in Christ (John 3:16), enter into Christ (Eph. 1:11–12), accept the judicial verdict of acquittal (Rom. 8:1), receive adoption alongside Christ (Rom. 8:15), "have access" through Christ (Eph. 2:18), come to Christ (John 6:37), and many more. All of them make the same point in a variety of ways. We and Jesus get together, and it is the start of a brand-new chapter of life.

I often find it a help at this stage of the discussion to take my friend to John 3:16, probably the best-known verse in the Bible. It stresses man's great need (perishing), God's great love (he even sent his Son), and the importance of making a decisive step of faith ("whoever believes in him"). My friend may well think that he does believe this already, so I take him back a page to John 1:12 to help him see what the Bible really means by believing. It is no vague mental assent. It is self-commitment on good evidence. John 1:12 expresses this by equating "believing" with "receiving." Those who believe in Jesus, those who receive him, can become children of God. It doesn't happen by blood—that is, you haven't always been a Christian, and you aren't a Christian because you were born in a Christian country. It doesn't happen by what John calls "the will of the flesh" (John 1:13 kjv): you can't earn it or work it up in yourself. It doesn't happen by the will of man: nobody else can get you into God's family, no pastor, no president, no parent. Only God can do it. It is his family. He welcomes you in—and he alone. Your part is to believe, or receive the gracious gift.

Your friend may "believe" about Jesus in his head, but never have "received" him into his life. His faith in Jesus may be intellectual, but not yet practical. It is very important to help him see the difference. Why not hold out some money to him and say, "Do you believe this is for you?" He will give you a wan smile and say yes without making a move. You reply, "Then you don't believe at all"—and withdraw the money! He will quickly appreciate the point: believing means receiving. It is only when he reaches out to grasp the money that it really becomes his. That is precisely what you are inviting him to do with God's divine gift, the Spirit of Jesus.

But how can that be done?

I often turn at this point to a third verse, alongside John 1:12 and 3:16. It is Revelation 3:20, a promise that has led millions to a personal faith. The imagery is so basic and so clear. It forms part of a communication from the risen Christ through his servant John to the church at Laodicea. The church is very formal. The members congratulate themselves, "I am rich, I have prospered, I need nothing"—a very modern illusion. They do not realize that they are "wretched, pitiable, poor, blind, and naked." But Christ offers to meet them in their need with "gold . . . that you may be rich; and white robes to clothe you and to keep the shame of your nakedness from being seen; and salve to anoint your eyes so that you may see" (Rev. 3:17–18 NRSV). Yet as things stand, Christ is the excluded party.

What a contradiction in terms—a Christless church! A church that has everything except Jesus. There are churches like that still. There are churches with people like that still. Jesus tells them that they need to make haste and repent. Then they need to receive him into their lives as they would a visitor into their home. "I stand at the door and knock. If anyone hears my voice and opens the door, I will come in and eat with him, and he with me" (Rev. 3:20). Jesus is the only one who can give new life and reality to this churchy but spiritually dead community. And he has been left outside, knocking. His hand is scarred. He died to win access to their lives. He longs to come in and make a difference if only they will let him. It is up to them. There is something to do—to let him in.

Your friend will probably see the point at once. He, too, has left Christ out of his life. He may well know about him, believe about him in his head, but he has never received him. He must open the door. He must ask him in. And the marvel of this particular image is that it is more than a picture. For when a person opens up to Christ, something happens. He is not the same as he was before. The Spirit of Christ has come in.

That image brought me to Jesus. Probably that is why I love it so much and use it so often. The Lord who made the house of our lives, the Lord who bought it back at such cost when it had been willfully wrenched from his ownership, stands knocking for admission. He is willing to come in and give the house a thorough spring cleaning and make repairs. He wants his light to shine out of the windows. But he will not act without the agreement of the tenant. That is the miracle of his humility and patience. He waits for us to ask him. Notice how the promise is unconditional. "I will come in." The offer is universal: "If anyone opens the door." What will your friend do with such an offer? Will he ask him in or keep him out? To respond to Jesus is urgent (Heb. 3:7–9). It is indispensable (Acts 4:12). It is unrepeatable (Heb. 10:14). Receiving Christ or making a commitment to Christ is, like marriage, instantaneous and unrepeatable. But like marriage, there is much that leads up to it and a lifelong adjustment that follows. Your friend needs to see clearly before making an informed decision. And it is to that step of commitment, and the problems often associated with it, that we turn in the next chapter.

6

Handling the Responses

The good news is dynamite. Many people remain in-
sulated from its impact for much of their lives, but
when they have had a conversation with you such as
the one suggested in the last chapter, they generally
see that they must do something about it.

Increasingly, these days, people are reluctant to
make a decision for Christ, certainly the first time they
have the challenge put to them. It often takes eight or
ten exposures to the gospel before they are ready. For
one thing, they sense there would be massive changes
of life involved. For another, they are not at all sure
that they believe it. And for another, it is, in the current climate, flying in the face of public opinion and
the attitudes and assumptions of most of their friends.
So we need to be patient and loving, but also ready to
help a friend handle the hesitations that crowd in at
such a time as this.

Your friend may have difficulty with any of the main
points you have been making.

DIFFICULTIES OVER REPENTANCE

You may well find that your friend has a problem here. He genuinely thinks he is all right as he is. How can you help him see the true situation?

I have found it very effective to take him through the most basic of moral codes, the Ten Commandments. If he hasn't kept these, he certainly has nothing to shout about before God. He will think, initially, that he has kept them all. But you may have to show him he has not kept any of them! Has he put God in the number one slot in his life? Of course not! Has he not made an image of God ("I can't believe in a God who . . . My idea of God is . . .")? Has he not taken God's name in vain, both by habitual blasphemy and by the much more serious hypocrisy, in all probability, of passing as a Christian, but having his heart far from the Lord? Has he given God any time—let alone a whole Sabbath day? No, God has been squeezed out of his timetable. And so you take him through all ten of them. If he is like me, he has not kept one. Honor Mom and Dad? You must be joking! No killing or adultery? Well, these are very much in fashion these days, but how can we look them in the face when Jesus traces murder back to hate in the heart and adultery back to unrestrained lust? Which of us can plead innocent on either count? Stealing from the Internal Revenue Service, vicious gossip about others, and destructive determination to grasp at all sorts of things we long for, but do not need. It's very up to date—and very humbling. What must God think about it?

I have often found that this journey through the Ten Commandments works powerfully with people who proudly think they are all right. Alternatively, I might do much the same with the Sermon on the Mount. Most people unthinkingly believe they have followed its teaching. But not a bit of it. Have they hungered and thirsted over what is right? Are they the pure in heart who alone will see God? Have they entered the narrow gate that leads to life, leaving behind the broad and well-populated road that leads to destruction? Do they seek first the kingdom of God and his righteousness? Of course not. The whole idea is ludicrous. But if they do not keep the life style of the kingdom, how can they possibly face the King?

I sometimes take a self-satisfied person through a passage like Romans 3:10–20. He is rarely so self-confident after that! James 2:10 has a logic that is armor piercing. If I am a generally law-abiding citizen and then am arrested for stealing, my general law-abiding-ness is no excuse, nor can it weigh in the balance against the charge. "Whoever keeps the whole law, and yet offends in one point, is guilty of the lot." Naturally, it makes sense with our legal system: it makes sense with God, too.

In all this, it is important to remember that you are not trying to arouse guilt over petty sins. You are trying to bring home to your friend the awesome guilt of keeping his Creator out of his life and running his life on auto rather than under the Maker's instructions. As Paul puts it, you want to encourage repentance toward God (Acts 20:21). He is the one who has been wronged and ignored. The friend, in common with the rest of us, has centered his life on himself; and God is calling for a change of direction, to center it on him. That is what is required in repentance. Only the Holy Spirit can convict of sin: you and I cannot do it. But as we gently expose a friend to what Scripture has to say, and pray while we do so, we can have quiet confidence that God will work upon his heart.

DIFFICULTIES OVER UNDERSTANDING

Very often the truth that seems so clear to you will remain obscure to your friend. You may need to go over it time after time, praying that the Holy Spirit will open his eyes to it. As Colin Day put it, "New questions are raised, and a further level to the answers given. The hope is that questioners will go on until they stumble across the pearl of great price as part of their search, or trip over, by accident, the treasure buried beneath their feet."

Your friend may still not understand what Jesus did for him on the cross. How could that death so long ago affect him personally? Show him that the offering of Jesus, who is *infinite,* more than covers the vast but finite number of people in the world. Show him that the cross is God's center point of history, where all the sins of all the sinners down the ages met—as if God took all that had happened in one hand and all that would happen before the end of history in the other, "and the LORD has laid [literally, made to meet] on him the iniquity of us all" (Isa. 53:6).

Maybe your friend still thinks he can earn salvation: the free grace of God is so very humbling to receive. Show him that not only is this impossible because we all do wrong things every day; it is also intolerable. God will not have his heaven spoiled by self-made men and women flaunting their supposed virtues. Heaven will be a place where we are "lost in wonder, love and praise" of the great God who stooped to rescue us. "By grace [i.e., God's free acceptance] you have been saved, through trusting him: not by your own achievements, lest anyone should boast" (Eph. 2:8–9, author's translation).

Maybe your friend has never understood the Resurrection. It means that Jesus is no history book figure;

he is alive and well, and it is possible to meet him. If your friend's intellect is unconvinced, take him through the Resurrection accounts in each of the four Gospels and 1 Corinthians 15. If you sense that fear of commitment is the trouble, tell him of the doubts you had; tell him of the leap of faith you made when you entrusted your life to the Risen One; tell him of the reality of that encounter and the difference Jesus has made. Testimony is powerful at this juncture.

DIFFICULTIES OVER COMMITMENT

It may well be, however, that your friend is not yet ready to entrust his life to Christ. It is a very big step, and commitment is not exactly one of the main characteristics of the late twentieth century. Men, in particular, are very wary about committing themselves to anything or anyone when they see it is going to be long term.

Of course, there may be some misunderstanding. He may confuse Christian commitment with an *intellectual agreement*. In that case, lead him to a verse like James 2:19 where the writer says, with biting irony, "You believe in one God: you are doing wonderfully well. The devils also believe—and tremble" (author's translation). That sort of belief is worthless: it does them no good. The devils believe the truth about God, but they do not commit themselves to his service. Is your friend going to join them?

Maybe he confuses real Christian commitment with some *emotional experience*. No, as Jesus puts it in Luke 11:13, it is receiving from God the Father the precious gift of the Holy Spirit—and there may be no emotional reaction to that at all, or it may be overwhelming.

Perhaps he is confused about *the sacraments*. They are meant to be pledges of commitment, like the wedding ring on the finger of the bride. But they can never be put forward as alternatives to commitment. You do not get married simply by putting a ring on your finger. That is part of it, but only part! Consequently, we are warned in Scripture against taking the outward symbol as a substitute for the inner reality it symbolizes and then preening ourselves on having it! Simon Magus took that attitude: he was baptized, yet he was not a true Christian. Peter said to him, "You have neither part nor lot in this [Christian] matter, for your heart is not right in the sight of God. . . . You are in the gall of bitterness and the bond of iniquity" (Acts 8:21, 23, author's translation). And Paul used an analogy from the Old Testament to drive home this truth that formalism is not enough: "He is not a Jew who is one outwardly, nor is true circumcision external and physical. He is a Jew who is one inwardly, and real circumcision is a matter of the heart, spiritual not literal" (Rom. 2:28–29, author's translation).

Or perhaps your friend is confused on the issue of *sudden decision:* he is not enthused about suddenness. Right: show him that it is not the date and time of his birth (natural or spiritual) that matter, but whether he is alive! Many people are alive all right, but do not know their birthday. It may take quite a long time for him to be clear that he has "passed from death to life," as the New Testament puts it. But most good things take time. It takes time for birth to happen—months of preparation, and the actual process takes many hours. No matter: the point is that whereas once there was no baby in the home, now there is. And that is far from being the end of the story: that baby will need to grow. But at least it is alive now! Evangelism is not about sudden conversions. I doubt if there is ever a really sudden one: always there are factors leading up to it and flowing from it. It is all about being in touch with

Jesus; it may be only a finger hold to start with, but that is contact. You can sense a person's reality and warmth and strength through even a finger hold. The strength of that grip will grow into a fierce embrace as the years go on. The important thing is to begin. "There is no condemnation to the person who is linked to Christ Jesus," exults Paul in Romans 8:1 (author's translation). It is the relationship with him, not the suddenness of it, that matters.

So there is often a measure of misunderstanding about commitment to Christ, but usually, most people understand it only too well. They simply can't bring themselves to do it! How can you help them? I have sometimes found the following ways useful.

You could say to your friend, "Fine. You don't feel ready yet. I fully respect that. What do you think is standing in your way? If we can sort that out to your satisfaction, would you then be ready to open your life to Christ?" And proceed from there.

Another person might respond better to some such approach as this: "Right, you feel you need more time? Great if you want to give the matter some mature reflection—but not so good if you want to postpone doing anything about it! Isaiah 55:6–7 has something relevant to say about that: 'Seek the LORD while he may be found; call on him while he is near.' So why not continue to think it over, and let's meet for a meal in a couple of days?" This approach respects your friend's desire for more time, but does not let him slip gently off the hook!

If you suspect that the reluctance about commitment is sheer evasion, a rather tougher approach might be in place: "You want to put it off? What would you say if someone for whom you had risked your life simply did not want to come and meet you to say, 'Thank you'? Would you not feel very hurt? How do you think Christ feels? He did not *risk* his life for you. He *gave* it.

In any case, it is foolish to keep him at arm's length. He wants to enrich your life, not rob you."

I have at times used all of these approaches to good effect, but it is crucial to be very sensitive to the unspoken things that are going on in your friend and to pray for divine wisdom as you seek to help him at this critical juncture.

Many other possibilities complicate the whole area of response to Christ for lots of people. For example, your friend may come from a *Catholic background.* It is best not to get involved in discussing doctrinal niceties at this point. Rather, stress the truths that may have been obscured by his background. His faith could be more in the Virgin Mary than in her Son. He may well be weak on grace and under the impression that if he goes regularly to Mass, all will be well. He may be weak, as many Catholics are, on God's assurance of salvation, in which case take him to the strong promises of God; Romans 5:1 and 8:1 are not a bad place to start. Sometimes I find with Catholics that they have all the framework of Christianity, but lack the picture in the middle of the frame—the picture of Jesus (especially Jesus risen and available). We do not need to disturb the frame: just insert the picture!

It may well be that your friend is indeed *a Christian, but quite unsure of it.* If so, he does not need decision; he needs assurance. I prefer to encourage him to look for the signs of spiritual reality in his life. He is meant to know where he stands (1 John 5:13), not to wallow in uncertainty throughout his life. The marks of new life, as outlined in John's first letter, are well worth going through with him. There will gradually emerge in a child of God a new sense of pardon, a new desire to please God, a new attitude to other people, a new love for other Christians, a new power over evil, a new joy and confidence, and a new experience of answered prayer (1 John 1:3–4; 2:1–2, 4, 6; 3:10; 4:4, 16–19;

5:14–15). Your friend is meant not just to feel or hope that he belongs, but to be sure of it, and these are some of the indicators.

Of course, when confronted with the challenge of radical change, your friend may come up with one of the classic difficulties or excuses. There is a fundamental difference between the two. The difference is this: if you manage to dispose of a real difficulty, then your friend will quite easily come to Christ—the barrier has been removed. But if you knock down an excuse, he will tend to produce another excuse and thus keep you at arm's length. So the genuine difficulty needs to be handled with sensitivity and care, whereas the excuse needs to be exposed for the unworthy thing it is. You will need to pray for a lot of wisdom and sensitivity as you try to help your friend at this point. Treat a difficulty as if it were a mere excuse, and you will cause deep hurt. Spend a lot of time answering a problem that is only a smoke screen, and you will get more smoke puffed in your face!

SOME COMMON EXCUSES

Common excuses include the following.

"I haven't got the time to go into it." The answer is, "Yes, you have. In this respect everyone is equal. We all have exactly the same amount of time—and we use it to prioritize the things we think important. What you mean is 'I don't think Jesus is important'—in which case it would be better for you and for everyone else if you came clean and said so."

"There are so many hypocrites in church" is often thrown at us. Well, there are. Nobody pretends the Christian church is sinless. But neither is your friend! So swallow down the temptation to say, "Come along and make one more" and try to prick the bubble by

asking him how many hypocrites he knows in the congregation and how he is so sure that they are hypocrites. Romans 14:12 is a valuable corrective to this excuse.

Another common excuse is *"I can be a Christian without going to church."* To this there is a very short answer: Jesus couldn't (Luke 4:16). But this whole attitude of minimalizing (how much can I get away *without* doing?) is the very antithesis of someone who has been really touched by the grace of God. Christianity is corporate, and it is generous. If that is his attitude, he has missed the genuine article.

Again, when you get to the point of challenging your friend to commit himself, you may well find him saying, to your astonishment, *"Well, I've always been a Christian."* That is just possible for someone born and raised in a loving Christian home, who has simply grown up with the Lord in an ever-deepening understanding and discipleship from earliest days. But generally when someone claims to have always been a Christian, take leave to doubt it! It is probable either that he is trying to pull the wool over your eyes or that he is identifying being a Christian with going to church (but see John 1:13; 2 Tim. 3:5), having been christened (but see Rom. 2:28; Acts 8:13–21), or doing his best (but see James 2:10; Matt. 22:37–39; Gal. 3:10). All these variations of the "I'm already a Christian" theme are generally excuses to conceal the real reason for his rebellion against God. That is what you will seek patiently and lovingly to unearth. Romans 1:18–32 is a devastating indictment of godless man in revolt, and is followed up by Romans 2, an equally shattering exposé of religious man in revolt!

Excuses such as these, and there are plenty more, generally spring from a mixture of pride and prejudice. They are fed by fashion, laziness, ignorance, fear, and materialism. These factors help to confirm our friends in their genial, undisclosed rebellion. The truly amazing thing is that God should continue to offer his pardon freely to those who are determined not to receive it (Rom. 5:6–10)!

SOME COMMON PROBLEMS

You will encounter a number of genuine difficulties as you try to help people at the point of commitment. Here are a few samples.

"Well, I will really make an effort to follow Christ" is the sort of thing you may hear from time to time. That attitude, though praiseworthy in a way, springs from the Pelagianism that lies so deep within us, the misguided illusion that we have a heart of gold! We always want to do rather than to receive. And the gospel is the good news of what God has done for us—something to be embraced, not earned. It is not try, but trust that lies at the heart of Christianity: not performance, but relationship. A lot of the New Testament is devoted to making this plain; verses such as Romans 4:3–5, Acts 16:31, and Isaiah 12:2 point it up.

"But I don't understand it all," some people will tell you—and this in the wake of your eloquent explanation! Of course, they don't understand it all! How could any mortal man fully understand what almighty God has done to make him acceptable? " 'What no eye has seen, nor ear heard, nor the human heart conceived, what God has prepared for those who love him' —these things God has revealed to us through the Spirit" (1 Cor. 2:9–10 NRSV). You do not need to understand electricity before you put the light on or the nutrient values of food before you eat it. "Taste and see that the LORD is good. Happy is the man who puts his trust in him" (Ps. 34:8, author's translation). Your job is to encourage your friends to entrust as much of

themselves as they are aware of to as much of Jesus as they understand. That is quite enough to establish realistic contact.

"I have tried it all before, and it is no good" is something that may come up. What is the "it" that he has tried? Is he confusing a deep turning to God with something less? Maybe he went forward at a crusade, but it never made any lasting difference? Perhaps his emotions were stirred, but his will remained untouched. Or maybe his decision was real, but he was never nurtured, never grew, and so gradually became indistinguishable from those who never began. Maybe he tried to go solo and avoided the Christian community: he has shriveled as a result. Maybe he never understood the power of the Holy Spirit in his life to break the grip of sinful habits. Maybe the chill winds of his own doubts and the skepticism of others have withered the tiny shoot of faith. You will need to exercise great care with this response. Show him that "if we are faithless, he [God] remains faithful—for he cannot deny himself" (2 Tim. 2:13 NRSV), and so, if he really opened up to Christ, Christ really came in—and build from there. Show him that his state depends not on his feelings but on the reliability of God, who has given us his word that "he who has the Son has life, and he who does not have the Son of God does not have life" (1 John 5:12). Has he or has he not welcomed the Son into his life? If he has, however long ago and however feebly done, Christ *has* come in. Feed him the promises of God. Let him learn some of them with you. They will prove invaluable as he launches out. But if, as he looks at his life, he concludes that he has never really begun the path of discipleship in earnest, then lead him to it as you would anyone else.

"I could never keep it up," your friend may observe. He's right. He couldn't. The whole point is that Christ will keep *him* up once he comes on board. Promises

such as John 10:28–29, 1 Peter 1:5, and Jude 24 make
that very plain. Once again, we are all driven back to
the unfamiliar but utterly necessary path of trust. It is
Christ's job to keep me from falling, but it is mine to
trust him to do so.

Perhaps the most common of all difficulties at the
point of decision is fear. *"I'm afraid."* That is honest
and not at all surprising. Help him to analyze that fear.
Is he afraid that nothing might happen? If so, take him
back to the Savior's promise, "I *will* come in." Jesus can
be trusted not to break his word. Is he afraid that he
will be letting himself in for a life of tedium and mis-
ery? Far from it: "In his presence there is fullness of
joy, and at his right hand there are pleasures forever-
more," as the psalmist knew (Ps. 16:11, author's translation). Is he scared of being in a minority? He will be,
but then one plus Christ is always a majority. Anyway,
since when has the majority always been right? Is he
afraid of what his friends would say? That is the usual
problem, and it is very real. Show him that any friends
who are worth their salt will not desert him. Show him
that he is not called to become a religious prig. Show
him that he is not required to drop any of his friends—
simply to be among them as before, but with Jesus just
beneath the surface of his life. Show him that perfect
love will cast out these fears of his (1 John 4:18) and
that he is about to welcome perfect love into his life.

THE STEP OF FAITH

The time has come when things seem pretty clear, and
the flow of questions has dried up a bit. Ask him
gently, "Do you think you are ready to say yes to the
Lord now? Or is there anything that is still keeping
you back from him?"

If he can't think of anything, say, "Right, then let's

kneel down right away and ask him to come into your life" (or whatever analogy you are using). Alternatively, you can ask him if he would prefer to make that solemn act of commitment on his own, and tell you when he has done so. Or would he like your presence and support at this important time? Mostly, I guess, he will opt for your help.

If so, sit or kneel next to him, pray for him, and then encourage him to pray for himself. The prayer may be short: "God, have mercy on me, a sinner." Jesus told us that was sufficient to send a man to his house justified (Luke 18:13–14). He may well want to build on the promise of Revelation 3:20 and ask the long-excluded Jesus to come in. He may, as in Luke 11:13, ask the Father to give the Holy Spirit to him. It is not so much the content of the prayer as the reality of the commitment that matters. But it is wise to encourage him, in any case, to ask the Lord to come and cleanse his past life, and put his Holy Spirit within.

It matters little whether he prays out loud (which he will probably never have done in his life) or silently. If he prefers the silent option, ask him to give you some indication of when he is through. You can then praise God for and with him. But it is often a good idea to encourage him to pray aloud. Tell him, "This doesn't mean God can't hear you if you pray silently; but I can't, and you wanted me to be alongside! Actually, I think it will help to seal the commitment if you do it out loud." Then he will usually do so with few inhibitions.

In either case, it is an enormous privilege to be alongside a friend at a time like this. The experience often moves me to tears. And then I pray for my friend, that the Holy Spirit will baptize him deeply into Christ, fill him with spiritual gifts, and never leave him.

It is generally a time of some emotion; tears and laughter often mingle in both of you. But it is important, in the sheer joy of the moment, not to omit vital things that need to be attended to.

THE IMMEDIATE SEQUEL

1. He needs to be clear where he stands. I generally turn to my friend and ask, "Did Jesus come in when you asked him?" In most cases he knows the answer without a shadow of doubt. But not always. In which case, I take him back again to the promise of Christ: "He says, 'If anyone opens the door I will come in.' Did you open the door?" "Well, yes, as best as I know how." "Then what has he done?" "Oh, I see, he *has* come in, even though I don't feel much different." "Precisely," I say. "You see, faith means trusting the faithfulness of Jesus, not your own volatile feelings. Jesus promised he would come in—not that you would immediately feel different!" And then I do with him what I would do with someone who is already happily sure. I encourage him to thank God for what has happened.

2. He needs to express his gratitude. He does not want to be like an ungrateful child, slow to give thanks for a generous present. So encourage a spirit of thankfulness in him from the start. Ask him to thank the Lord for coming in. And this time, there is hardly ever any problem about praying out loud: "Dear Lord, thank you so much for coming into my life. Thank you for your promise that you will never leave me. Help me to be true to you all through the rest of my life." A prayer like that is an early lesson for your friend. He needs to come to the Lord with gratitude and praise, not just with requests.

3. He needs initial protection against doubt. Doubts always crowd in after someone has made a commitment to Christ. Was it real? Was I just an emotional fool? Will it last? What happens when I do something wrong? You would be wise not to attempt anything comprehensive at this stage, but it is good to send him away with just one promise of Christ in his mind. I often use 1 John 5:12: "He who has the Son has life; he who does not have the Son of God does not have life." Does he have the Son? Why, yes, if he has invited him into his life. Then he *has* God's life, God's eternal life in him. I get him to repeat it several times with its reference and maybe mark it in a New Testament that I give him. Warn him that doubt is Satan's prime weapon against the new believer. If he cannot keep your friend from becoming a Christian, he will do his best to make sure he does not enjoy it and is not sure about it! And the sooner the new Christian learns, like his Master, to face doubt with the promises of Scripture and say, "It is written," the sooner he is likely to find his feet as a Christian and grow.

4. He needs to tell someone else. The New Testament insists in a variety of ways that we need to confess with our mouths that we belong to Jesus, and not just believe in him secretly in our hearts. Show him that very point in Romans 10:9–10. He will find it difficult initially, but an enormous help in the long run, to go and tell someone else the commitment he has made. Encourage him to find someone who will be glad to hear it! Probably, he is aware of someone who has been praying for him for some time. What a joy it will be for that person when he goes and tells him or her! If he is a youngster at home, he might be wise to let his life speak for a while before trying to say anything to his parents (and getting put down). But given that proviso, he needs to go public to somebody soon; and it will be a great strengthening in his own life when he does so.

5. He needs tender loving care. And very soon. The enemy will be at work, seeking to destroy a fledgling Christian life. So you must be at work, helping him to see what strength and riches he has inherited in Christ. He has had quite enough for one day, but book him up there and then to come and see you in a day or two, when you can help him with the early problems he will run into and begin to show him how to grow in the life of discipleship. Meanwhile, give him a booklet like *Becoming a Christian* by John Stott, *Why Jesus?* by Nicky Gumbel, or my *Come, Follow Me* to take away, read, and reflect on as he enters the most exciting of all relationships, with Jesus Christ as his Savior and Lord.

7

Offering the Aftercare

One of the weakest aspects of the Western church is our failure to give proper aftercare to people who profess faith. Maybe it is because we do not expect to see many new adult believers. Maybe it is because we assume that Christian education ends, for all intents and purposes, when an adolescent is received into full church membership at a ceremony that many of them seem to treat as an event indicating that training is over. Yet the nurture of new adherents is an area to which the first Christians gave tremendous care, even in the earliest period of the apostolic age. We have not only the explicit insistence of the book of Acts on the subject, but traces of the actual teaching they gave to new converts remain in the New Testament letters. Today, however, it is a very neglected area. New Christians are expected to join a church and to fit in. They must sink or swim.

And many of them sink. A drift away from the churches is gaining momentum. They are felt to be boring. Their worship is seen as culturally inappropriate. They do not seem to connect very well with Monday-to-Saturday life. And the teaching does not scratch people where they itch. No, it simply will not do to suppose that your friend will survive happily if you take him to church. For the culture gap between the church and the rest of society is widening all the time. The books, the music, the assumptions about the world and God and life style—all are so different in church circles from what the ordinary nonreligious person is used to. So he or she is being asked to make a massive cultural shift by going to church, which may be even more difficult than entrusting one's life to Christ.

The church is very much to blame in this matter. For years those of us in the church have taken little or no trouble to be user-friendly, and we cannot be surprised if people find it really threatening to cross our thresholds. There is even a smell about a church that is unattractive! Many of our churches have lost the outward thrust that they should have if, as William Temple asserted, "the church is the only society in the world which exists for the benefit of the non-member." We are organized not so much for outreach as for maintenance. Naturally, therefore, it is going to be hard for someone not brought up in the church to fit into most congregations these days.

What then is to be done?

Following Jesus is a lifetime's job. One of the most common names for it in the New Testament is to become a "disciple," a "learner." What we need to learn is a growing relationship with Jesus that will progressively infect our whole lives. Christian living is not about rules and regulations: if it were, it would become a new legalism (and that is what it is perilously like in some churches).

No, your friend has been called to a new liberation. It is like falling in love with the most wonderful person in the world. You would do anything to please that person as the relationship develops. But you do it out of love, not out of the rule book.

There is nobody who can help your friend into the

life of discipleship better than you. Others may know more, and be more experienced, but they will not be nearly as much use. For you are his friend. You are the person who introduced him to Jesus. You have a unique entrée. He will take things from you that he would never take from anyone else. He needs you as much as Paul, when he was a new Christian, needed to be taken under the wing of Barnabas. He needed tender, loving, personal care in the early weeks of discipleship before being introduced to the church. Take it slowly with your friend: not too much too soon. At the heart of it there is your friendship with him. You are alongside to help him to learn.

Very well, what aspects of learning are important for the new disciple? Here are eight that come to mind:

1. *Learning to be confident* is an essential part. Not the arrogance that is so unattractive, but the quiet confidence of a team member who knows she has been selected, the confidence of a child who knows he is in the family. You gave your friend the initial grounds of assurance when you helped him to Christ. He needs to trust the promise of the Jesus who cannot lie. Christian confidence rests entirely in God. God the Father assures us we are accepted in his family (Rom. 8:15). God the Son accepted our guilt on the cross, and now "we have peace with God through our Lord Jesus Christ" (Rom. 5:1). And God the Holy Spirit gradually makes his presence felt by the changes he brings about in our lives. They are laid out carefully, as we have seen, in the first letter of John. There is a new sense of pardon. There is a new desire to please God. There is a new attitude of caring about other people. There is a new love for fellow Christians. There is a new power over evil. There are a new joy and a new confidence. There is a new experience of answered prayer. "Look," he says, "I make all things new!" It does not happen all

at once, but gradually these things appear in the life, like spring flowers out of frozen earth.

2. *Learning to listen to God* is a significant part of discipleship, and one that will be new to him. He may have said his prayers prior to entrusting his life to Christ, but that is talking, not listening. You can never learn from someone unless you listen to him. How can your friend learn to listen to God? The Bible is one of the main ways. We are not left without an instruction manual for this Christian life. The manual has little interest for us until we start a life of discipleship. But once we do, it becomes vital. Yet it is different from all other manuals. It is not written instructions; it is a sort of love letter from God to us. It contains warnings, encouragements, terrible mistakes believers have made, exciting stories, letters, and four wonderful interpretations of Jesus. It will be your privilege to introduce this Bible (which is more like a library than a single book) to your friend. It may be very new to him. It may be quite familiar. In either case, you will help him to read it in an entirely fresh way: not as literature, but as a meeting point with God. It will mean reading a passage over to see its main thrust, and saying to himself, "I wonder how that affects me." It will mean reading it again for a promise to claim, an example to follow, an encouragement to revel in, a challenge to face, a prayer to use, or simply something new about the Lord. It will be your joy to read a bit of Scripture with your friend and show him how to meditate on it, to chew it over and draw out its sweetness. There is no bibliolatry, no worship of the Bible in all this. Martin Luther long ago observed that just as we only go to a cradle in order to find the baby, so we only go to the Scriptures in order to find the Christ. Augustine called Scripture a letter from home, and that is the attitude to inculcate in your friend as he begins with you to read a bit of it.

I suggest you meet him once a week to begin with, and choose a passage that will not only enable you both to draw thoughts from it, but will take a major topic of the Christian faith as its subject matter. On the first occasion, for example, you might take John 3:1–16 or Luke 19:1–10 and study it as an example of initial commitment to Jesus. The next week you might take Luke 11:1–13 on prayer. The next week you could do Matthew 4:1–11 on Scripture and discuss how Jesus used it in a practical way to counter temptation. And so on. And all the time you will be showing your friend how to listen to God as he begins to draw thoughts from the passage, reflects on them quietly, and turn them into prayers or praises—out loud with you. This will give him a model to use in his private reading of the Bible, which you can encourage through giving him some notes to help him, such as the Scripture Union or the Bible Reading Fellowship provides.

3. *Learning to pray* is a vital and closely allied part of discipleship. A lover who never communicates would be a strange creature; so would a prayerless disciple. Unfortunately, there are a lot of them around. No doubt your friend does not want to be one of them. Some estimates suggest the average Christian spends only a minute or two a day in prayer. Prayer is really a new dimension of life: sharing everything with the Lord. It involves asking, of course: everyone understands that. It involves saying, "Thank you"—far less obvious to many. It involves quiet meditation over Scripture and its application to life and our relationship with God. It involves silently just looking up into his face. It involves awe and wonder: "Lord, you are wonderful." It involves confession. When we go wrong, we need to come back at once to the Lord and confess it and get it put out of the way: "Forgive us our trespasses" is an essential part of the disciple's prayer life.

You will show your friend how to turn thoughts from his Bible reading into prayers for his own devotional life. You will encourage him to make a simple list of issues he wants to bring regularly before the Lord—things at work, in the home, on the world scene. You will help him to see himself as God's bridgehead into situations where he has an influence, in the family, in the workplace, in leisure activities, and to begin to pray for the main people he meets in those areas. Before long he will see some remarkable answers and get excited; prayer will be not so much an activity, more a way of life. And it is one you can share with him as you meet him regularly and ensure that part of your time together is devoted to praise and intercession.

I am a shameless advocate of praying with people at all sorts of odd moments if they so desire: an arm around a friend on the street and a brief prayer, prayer before going home after an evening out with your friend, a quick prayer when some bad news or a new challenge comes. In this way, you will be encouraging your friend to abide in Christ as naturally as a branch does in a tree—drawing resources from the Lord almost without thinking about it, because it has become second nature to share everything with him. And Jesus promised that when we do abide in him like that, there will be joy and fruitfulness. His life will begin to show through, just as the sap of the tree shows itself in the leaves and fruit of the branch.

4. *Learning to raise problems* is an important part of every child's development, and it is just as important for the young Christian. Here again, your presence and friendship are crucial. If you have that regular time once a week or so with the friend you have led to faith, and if you inquire gently about how things are going, you will find all manner of issues emerging—things that are on his mind. Often you will be able to help

because you faced that issue some time ago. Sometimes his doubts will echo some of yours—and you must be very frank about your doubts. This should show him two things. First, that to have doubts on many things is quite compatible with a deep assurance about belonging to Christ. And second, that doubts are not shameful things to be hidden but things to be talked openly about with friends. All of this will develop a natural inquiring spirit about his Christianity so that it does not become a clone of your own. And it will save him from giving it all up after vainly trying to hide doubts that he imagines Christians should not have!

Looking back to the early days of my adult discipleship, I reckon that the regular time of meeting the person who led me to Christ, and throwing my doubts, questions, and failures at him, helped me more than almost any other factor into mature discipleship. We all need a soul friend with whom we can share in depth.

5. *Learning to face the music* is part of discipleship. Jesus made it very plain that following him was tough. It would mean being in a minority. It would mean standing up for truth when it was very unfashionable. It would mean putting allegiance to him before other relationships. It would mean, above all, that we encounter the full force of that trinity of evil: the world, the flesh, and the devil. All three will tend to drag him down. "The world" means society organized without reference to God, and we all know what a pull that has through the peer group, political correctness, racist or sexist attitudes, and our fear of stepping out of line. Then there is the pull of "the flesh," the self-oriented life, the temptations that have become like old friends because we have given in to them so long. You will need to help him there. And behind the pressures, from outside the Christian and within, there is an organizing force of evil that the Bible calls "the devil."

Your friend may not believe in the devil: he is not an article of Christian faith! But he will soon discover the devil's reality and power. And the way to win against all three pressures is the same. It is easy to understand but difficult to achieve. I never heard it put more clearly than this: *I can't overcome temptation. Christ can. I can by trusting him.*

You need to help your friend develop this trusting. Trusting Jesus to change the corrupt desires of our hearts. Trusting him to give us courage to stand against the run of public opinion when need be. Trusting him to give us needed strength when we turn to him in the moment of temptation and mutter, "Help!" This will all take time. It is also hard because it is so unnatural for us to depend on someone else, and not just on our own resources—even when that someone is Jesus. So there will be lots of failures as your friend discovers how strong are the forces of evil that he has a new desire to defeat, and how hard he finds it to trust Christ when temptation strikes. Failures, like ink stains, need to be dealt with immediately before they soak in! Don't let your friend be dismayed that things get more difficult once he has become a disciple. He has become a live fish swimming against the current, whereas beforehand he was a dead one, floating downstream with all the rest. Temptation is not sin: he needs to recognize that. Giving in to it is.

6. *Learning to live for others* is another part of Christian discipleship. Some years ago, the title "Man for Others" was in common use about Jesus, and though inadequate, it points up a vital aspect of his life. It was poured out for other people. And in this materialist and basically selfish society, few things speak more eloquently for Jesus than sheer benevolence to others, giving without thought of anything in return. I shall not forget the amazement at a checkout line in a supermarket when I heard the person in front of me say with

dismay, "Oh, I can't pay for all that." So I said, "I'd be glad to make up the difference," and I did. It seemed a natural thing to do, and I had no idea that it would have any repercussions. But months later, when I went back to that store, I found the employees remembered me as the person who had paid someone else's bill! A tiny thing to do but unusual enough these days to cause comment.

It will be your job to excite your friend with the truth of Jesus' words: "it is happier to give than to get." That flies in the face of the world's values, but it lies at the heart of discipleship. Every Christian knows John 3:16, but 1 John 3:16–18 is just as important! "This is how we know love. He laid down his life for us, and we ought to lay down our lives for the brethren." John continues, "If anyone has the world's goods and sees his brother in need, yet closes his heart against him, how does God's love abide in him? Little children, let us not love in word or speech, but in deed and truth" (author's translation).

Curiously enough, this learning to live for others is very closely related to one of the biggest hungers of our time. People are realizing that materialism by itself does not give deep satisfaction. Moreover, the money market is highly volatile, and jobs are increasingly scarce. People want to design their lives so as to gain maximum satisfaction. Leisure activities and private associations figure far more prominently than they used to in our priorities; and above all is the longing for relationships. And when we start seriously learning to live for others, we discover a marvelous fulfillment of those longings, though in a paradoxical way. Jesus said, "Whoever tries to hang on to his life will lose it; and whoever is willing to give his life away for my sake and the gospel's will find it" (Mark 8:35, author's translation). It seems improbable, but it is true. The Christian prescription of living for others is, curiously enough, the highway to discovering the very thing modern man is longing for —deep satisfaction.

7. *Learning to belong* is another fundamental aspect of discipleship into which you will need to lead your friend. Jesus called his disciples individually, but he called them into a group. Christianity is inescapably corporate. All the images of Christians in the Bible show that corporate nature. We are limbs in a body, soldiers in an army, guests at a banquet, stones in a building. We need each other. And that, too, flies in the face of the sturdy independence that most people aim for. The truth is, of course, that we cannot cope on our own. We are not islands, but all part of the mainland. We need each other if we are to grow in our humanity, discover our special giftings, and become a useful force in society. Western individualism, reinforced by inadequate evangelism, fosters the myth that we are still part of the "me" generation. Not so. Christians belong to the "us" generation, and the sooner your friend learns it, the happier he will be in the Christian life. The church, in a word, is not an optional extra for Christians. We are born again into it. We belong.

Now it may be that your friend is so alienated from Christian things that it would be a mistake to try to get him straight into church. Nevertheless, he does need to be introduced as soon as possible to Christian fellowship. It could begin with meeting a couple of your Christian friends over a meal, ending up with your praying a bit together, and maybe singing praise to God with a guitar and a verse of Scripture set to a simple tune. I think of an occasion on a mission when we saw a number of young offenders turn to Christ. They would have been totally lost in a local church, so we set up a sort of halfway house for them to settle into for six months or so, led by a very sensitive older

Christian well acquainted with prison culture. It worked well.

But perhaps the best form of Christian fellowship for a new believer is a small group of three or four others who have recently come to faith or are seriously thinking about it. These groups are increasingly common: you find them under the names of Nurture Groups, Discovery Groups, Cell Groups, and the like. No matter the name, the idea is much the same: to provide, in the warmth and hospitality of a Christian home, the context in which an inquirer can get to the point of commitment and a new Christian can grow. They have enormous advantages. Competent leadership is offered by an experienced couple who are warm and laid-back and don't talk too much. The members share with the group where they are spiritually. They rapidly discover the joy of fellowship around Christ and the Scriptures. They learn to pray informally and briefly in their own words among others so disposed. They can ask questions about the problems of belief and behavior they are bound to encounter. They will see each other growing and be stimulated by it. And these groups prepare their members for belonging to a house group in the local church when the Nurture Group is over. It is, if you like, a nursery for the newly born. Every church needs a nursery, especially if it is looking for new births.

But having a nursery does not mean that you cease to bear any responsibility for your friend. The best of all courses of action would be for you to be one of the leaders of the Nurture Group, because in these groups it is not just the weekly meeting that is on offer, but occasional pastoral sessions with a leader. And if you are that leader, you can combine your one-on-one care of your friend with watching and helping him to grow in the fellowship of the group.

Churchgoing will become so much easier if your

friend has joined one of these groups. Group partici-
pants go together to a service and will be able to share
impressions and raise problems with their group leaders afterward. Gradually, the new believer does need to
become an active member of the local church. His
presence will encourage those who have been there for
ages: it will also provide fresh oxygen in the waters of
worship that may have been getting a bit stale. The
issue of baptism needs to be talked over with the minister. So does full church membership, and you need to
discover what are the rules of the denomination for his
taking part in the central service of the Christian
church, the holy Communion.

8. *That leads me* naturally to the last of the initial
learning steps I want to emphasize: last, but not least.
It is worship. *Learning to worship* is a fundamental part
of being a Christian. The word literally means "worth-
ship," and in all true worship we lose ourselves in awe
and love and praise of the great God who has bothered
about people like us. We want to extol his worth. That
is the honor he deserves. It cuts us down to size, too,
which is a constant necessity! And regular worship becomes the center point of the week, which brings a
balance and a perspective to all else.

The instinct to worship is deeply rooted in human
beings; the trouble is, it is misdirected when we leave
God out. The worshiping spirit in secular society is
directed to football and basketball players, film stars,
royalty, or some other object we want to honor because it takes us out of our selves, our pettiness, and
our selfishness. Now that your friend has come to
Christ, he is able to fulfill that instinct in a way that
was never possible before. He can pour out his love
and adoration on the God who made the world and yet
humbles himself to care about the least details of our
lives. The new *Anglican Prayer Book* (the Alternative
Service Book 1980) explains the purposes of worship

very clearly, at the outset of its morning and evening services:

> We have come together as the family of God
> in our Father's presence
> to offer him praise and thanksgiving,
> to hear and receive his holy word,
> to bring before him the needs of the world,
> to ask his forgiveness of our sins,
> and to seek his grace [i.e., help],
> that through his Son Jesus Christ
> we may give ourselves to his service.

The central act in Christian worship is the Lord's Supper, Eucharist, or holy Communion. It is central because it is the one thing Jesus told his followers to do in remembrance of him. He did not leave us a set of rules, an organization, or even a book. He left us a meal! Isn't that wonderful? Fellowship around a table is about the closest thing we human beings can enjoy together. And if that fellowship has Jesus as the focus, Jesus as the host, no wonder the worship is profound. You may find it a help to explain to your friend some of the aspects of this wonderful service. In it we look *in* at ourselves and confess the things that have gone wrong. We look *back* to Calvary and praise Jesus for his death for us. We look *up* to his risen presence, longing to nourish us through the bread and wine that he said were his body and blood. We look *around* in love and fellowship with the other guests at God's table. We look *forward* to his return at the end of all history, the marriage supper of the Lamb, of which every Communion is a foretaste. And then we look *out* to a needy world; the Communion is battle rations for Christian soldiers.

So there is a lot of learning to be done. It all takes time; indeed, it won't be completed in a lifetime. That's what heaven is for. So do not expect too much of your friend, especially in the early days. "Tender loving care" and "Not too much too soon" are good maxims in these days when Christianity is increasingly obscure to the majority of our population, and many of them have to contend with massive problems, including coming from broken homes where they have never experienced love without strings attached. It takes time for street kids to assimilate to the life style of a royal palace, even after they have received the adoption certificate! But your job is to help the process along. It is a very great privilege. "We are God's fellow workers; you are God's field" (1 Cor. 3:9).

8

Avoiding the Mistakes

The Romans had three words for it: *humanum est errare* (It is only human to make mistakes). And that is certainly the case in talking to our friends about Christ. In this final chapter I want to warn against some of the mistakes that I have made or have seen other people make as we have tried to point people to Jesus.

TALKING TOO MUCH

Any evangelist you know is almost sure to be a talker. It seems to be a matter of temperament. I suppose that someone with an outgoing, relaxed temperament, once won to Christ, is likely to be a good communicator of the gospel. But the person who talks too much can be a major turnoff, particularly for shy or sensitive people. They would respond much better to a quieter, more hesitant presentation. Not too glib. Not too many words. No trace of overconfidence. The introvert is likely to react against someone who talks too much and comes on strong. That is one reason why extroverts are by no means always the best evangelists. If you are low-key and avoid any trace of exaggeration, you may well get through to a person who shies away from the easy talker.

Perhaps nervousness is the trouble, but there is an undeniable tendency for us to talk too much when we are trying to share the good news with a friend. Like good doctors, we need to diagnose before we prescribe. We need to see where the friend is living in his inner life. There has to be an honest and relaxed dialogue. We are far from the mark if we imagine that people have empty heads and that once we have learned how to pry the lids off, then we can pour in the contents of the gospel. As Haddon Robinson put it:

> Heads are neither open nor hollow. Heads have lids, screwed on tightly, and no amount of pouring can force ideas inside. Minds only open when their owners sense a need to open them. Even then, ideas must still filter through layers of experience, habit, prejudice, fear and suspicion. If ideas make it through at all, it is because feedback operates between speaker and listener.

You have only to think of your reaction to the Jehovah's Witnesses couple at the door to see what he means. We do not open our minds to that sort of invasion. It is not for us. So if we persist in speaking when a friend does not want to hear, we will alienate him. It is much better to move easily on and off the subject of the gospel as the conversation opens up and as he wants to pursue it. Use lots of questions. Find out his views and respect them, agreeing with them wherever you can. Only two-way communication is going to have a lasting impact.

TALKING TOO LITTLE

If the fervent evangelist is tempted to talk too much, many of us are tempted to talk too little about Christ to our friends. We feel embarrassed to raise the subject. The friend might be offended. We might even lose the friendship. Initially, we put it off, saying to ourselves, "I must get to know him better first." Then we give up on it, saying to ourselves, "It might spoil the relationship." Surely, the right balance is to make certain that as we gradually disclose ourselves to the people who are becoming our friends, we are never embarrassed to admit our Christian allegiance, but we never press it on them. Let it unfold naturally as part of the person they are getting to know. The opportunities will emerge later, and by then we have earned the right to speak.

I remember hearing of a couple of men who played golf together every week. They talked of almost everything under the sun. But they did not talk about Jesus, although one of them was a Christian. Time came when the non-Christian lay on his deathbed, and the Christian friend tried to talk to him about Jesus. "Forget it, John," he said. "If it had been that important, you would have talked about it years ago." Talking too little to our friends can be as disastrous as talking too much.

FAILING TO GET ALONGSIDE

What you believe and live by is a very personal matter, and people are not keen to have it corrected by absolute strangers. We have to get alongside folks if we are to have any hope of introducing them to Jesus. Dr. John Drane tells a macabre story about this sort of failure. He was walking with his little daughter in a park, watching the squirrels and kicking piles of dead leaves. And then, with the directness of a child, she asked, "Daddy, do you think God is at the bottom of everything?" While he was deciding how to reply, a middle-aged man jumped out of the bushes and demanded, "Young man, are you saved?" Giving John a minisermon and a warning to think about these things before it was too late, he disappeared into the bushes again, leaving the little girl to ask, "Daddy, what did that man want?" It was, says John Drane, much harder to give a satisfactory answer to that question than to the first one she had asked! Shotgun, nonrelational evangelism was an appalling intrusion, just as father and daughter, on the basis of love and trust, were discussing the very meaning of life! That's the damage insensitive evangelism can do.

We all get fed up with the golf bore or the fishing bore. It is all too easy to become Christian bores if we fail to really get inside a friend's outlook and interests. We must try to put ourselves in his shoes. What would he want to hear about Jesus that would really interest him? How could we express it in the most imaginative way? How could we avoid the language of Zion and church forms of expression that put so many people off? I was intrigued to discover from a recent survey of British churchgoers that 42 percent admitted to falling asleep in church, and 67 percent sometimes wished they had stayed in bed on Sunday morning instead of going to church. I am amazed at the number of ministers worldwide who seem to succeed in making Jesus, the most exciting person the world has ever seen, dull! But I wonder if in my enthusiasm to talk about him, I sometimes bore my friends with one-track communication. If so, I have failed to get alongside. Think of Jesus really getting alongside the woman at the well. Think of him getting alongside the two friends on the road to Emmaus. In each case, he listens. In each case, he tells them good news, but it is good news relevant to the topic uppermost in their minds.

STARTING WITH GUILT

I was brought up in the early days of my Christian discipleship to see the heart of the good news as a three- or four-point presentation, of which human sinfulness was the opening salvo. I have come to see that this is not the right way to proceed. Indeed, a lot of people these days do not have any sense of guilt until they have been Christians for some time. It is not the universal way in, nor is it the best—true though it is that "all have sinned and come short of the glory of God." In Luther's time, as among the Jews of Paul's day, *guilt* was a superb doorway for the gospel. If you believe strongly in ethical monotheism, you do not have to be a profound thinker to realize that you have blown it comprehensively and are in severe difficulty. "How shall a man be right with God?" is your problem, and Jesus is the marvelous, undreamed-of answer to that question. In Victorian days, *life after death* dominated people's minds. Preaching majored, in those days, on heaven and hell. But that is not where people are at today. Modern Western men and women are plagued by *meaninglessness* and the apparent lack of purpose in the world; by the problem of *suffering,* which they see projected every night on their TV screens; by *relationships,* which are the most precious things in life and yet get the most snarled up. These, then, are the ways in for the modern preacher—and for the friend who wants to commend Jesus.

Instead of starting with guilt, there is a lot to be said for starting with *affirmation.* That is what Paul did at Athens, "I perceive that you are very religious" (paraphrase), or at Pisidian Antioch, "Men of Israel and you Godfearers, listen. The God of this people Israel chose our fathers" (paraphrase). The Bible begins not with the fall of man, but with the God who made all things good; and there are traces of that goodness in everyone. Let's try to link up with it, not come in heavily in a judgmental fashion. They know they have done wrong. They anticipate condemnation from the church. They feel they are not good enough. Let's surprise them. Let's show them first and foremost the love of God to humans. Isn't that love the heart of it all? Should we not start with that rather than human failure?

MAKING RATIONALISTIC ARGUMENTS

It is ironic that evangelical Christians, while deploring the rationalism of the Enlightenment, often give way to it themselves. Books written with the best of motives, like Josh McDowell's *Evidence That Demands a Verdict* and Norman Geisler's *Christian Apologetics,* get dangerously near to trying to argue people into the kingdom of God, as if it were just a matter of winning the debate. Of course, that will never do if only because the heart has its reasons of which the mind knows nothing. People are more often held back from God by fear or substance abuse than by having inadequate proofs for the existence of God or the truth of the Resurrection. Of course, there is a place for plain speaking on these topics. And the unbelievers certainly do not have all the best arguments. But we must never forget that it is easy to win the argument and lose the person we are trying to help. We are looking for that new birth from above, which no human being can orchestrate. There is a proper place for apologetics, and it is to remove stumbling blocks on the way to Christ, like a bulldozer when a landslide blocks the road. But it does little toward getting your friend to Christ. He has to make that journey on his own. You can clear the road of obstacles, but he has to set out. So there is no way we

can evade the challenge of love and prayer and patience.

Having said that, rationalistic arguments are even
less effective now than they have ever been. The current postmodernism has little time for such argumenta-
tion, seeing it as part of the old ways that proved so
barren. The feel-good factor, "what works for me"—
these are today's concerns. It is wise, therefore, not to
neglect the truth issues, but to major on those experi-
ential aspects of the good news that most appeal to
your friend. Jesus the friend, Jesus the conqueror of
death, the Jesus who makes sense of life, who will
never fire us like any other employer—these are the
gospel tendrils that will draw modern people to him.
The attractiveness of the good news, rather than the
judgment that comes from rejecting it, should be our
main suit. We must never gloss over human sin, but it
does not need to be the first issue we raise! The gospel
does satisfy the head, but it meets the longings of the
heart, too, and it is with those that modern men and
women are most immediately concerned.

MAKING THE GOSPEL SHALLOW

I am afraid a good deal of this goes on in some circles
today. Some people make the gospel *entirely individual-
istic.* It is presented in terms of personal sin and personal salvation. It is all about where you go if you die
tonight. That is legitimate and there is a place for it,
but it falls very far short of full-blooded Christianity,
which has a cosmic dimension, embracing past, present, and future, embracing man and his environment,
embracing the individual and the new humanity of
which he becomes a part.

Or else it is presented in terms of a *sudden decision* to
accept Christ without giving any realistic indication of

what needs to follow or the cost of discipleship. "May I see a hand in the air? Thank you. And another in the gallery!" We have all heard that sort of thing. It is unworthy in preachers and should be a warning to us, in our one-on-one conversations with our friends, to avoid a shallow presentation of the good news. It will not have a lasting impact; indeed, it will do a lot of harm.

I recall with embarrassment a man called John whom I helped to trust Christ while we were both first-year students at Oxford. I was very distressed to return after our first vacation and find that he had gone back on his profession to follow Christ. "Michael," he said, "you never told me how much it would cost." Well, I had told him how much it would cost. But I had obviously not made it plain to him. I hope I learned a lesson that day that I have never forgotten. Never pull your punches in the hope of a quick decision. You—and your friend—will rue the day.

Another regrettably shallow style of evangelism is to see it as simply *saving the soul* of the friend to whom we are witnessing. Saving souls is more the stuff of a certain type of propaganda than of the New Testament. The "save" language, in both Hebrew and Greek, has a very this-worldly side to it, and it is certainly not only, or even primarily, concerned with our destination after death. It has links with healing, with victory over enemies, with handling fear and loneliness. It is a very big word; and it is applied to *people,* not some abstract *soul.* Once we see this, it becomes apparent that food and medicine, friendships and even housing may well need to be part of the message of salvation. After all, our gospel is about a God who left the invisible spiritual realm in order to incarnate himself among us. Our presentation of him must not neglect that strongly material aspect and soar off into what we are pleased to call the spiritual. During the past eighty years or so, there has been a disastrous split between conservative Christians who preached to people and liberal Christians who did good things for them. Mercifully, we now appreciate that both are important!

The good news is all-embracing. Let us not become gospel shrinkers!

CREATING A NEW BONDAGE

Our message is about the liberation Christ brings, but sometimes we contradict that message by the way we go about it.

Some people are so wedded to one particular way of telling the gospel that it comes over as a sort of steel framework through which a friend must crawl. It may be the four spiritual laws or the ABCs of salvation or whatever. The impression is given that this is *the* way to Christ, and the friend had better follow it. Of course, this approach has no basis in the Scriptures, where there is a rich variety of avenues to Christ. In his own dealings with individuals, Jesus is never once recorded as having repeated himself. All these memory aids that people concoct have a value in helping us to remember some of the salient elements in the good news. But they have become disastrous if we try to put everyone through the same hoop. It is not liberty, but a new bondage we are expressing, even though we may not realize it.

There is another aspect to this new bondage. A sad fact is that it, too, is found in some Christian circles. As soon as a person professes faith, he or she is assailed with a lot of taboos (do not gamble or drink alcohol), new regulations (you must read your Bible every day), and customs (church on Sunday, preferably in a suit). This is often most noticeably the case in denominations that pride themselves on being free from the traditions of mainline churches! These rules are meant, of course, to be hedges around the field of Christian freedom, but they all too easily turn into a prison. Ask yourself if the average Christian displays more or less true freedom and flexibility of mind and life style than his neighbor who makes no Christian profession. We must not be blacksmiths, forging new chains for people. We need to apply the acetylene torch that sets them free.

EXERTING WRONG PRESSURE

Having been present at a great many evangelistic occasions, I confess that I have become very suspicious of the human pressure that I have seen exerted by the speaker. It verges sometimes on manipulation of people's feelings. It is wrong in itself, for this is God's work, not ours. And it has the most terrible payoff: people can be wounded for life through undue pressure by an ardent evangelist.

Deep down it comes from our failure to trust the Lord; we assume that the response should be *now,* and that *we* should be the ones to bring it about. But did not Jesus tell Nicodemus that the wind of the Spirit blows where it will, and you cannot chart its direction or know its source? We need to tell the good news like it is. We need to add our testimony to its truth and power. We need to show a friend that there is a decision to be made. But we must not press. It is the Holy Spirit's job to bring him to the point of saying, "Jesus is Lord"—not ours. Remember even Jesus let the rich young ruler walk away.

So we must not think we have failed if a friend does not respond at once. We must get out of the mentality of spilling the whole thing on him in one go, expecting

instant results. Little by little does it, relying on God to
make his breakthrough at the right time.

Having warned against exerting wrong man-made
pressure at a delicate point in a friend's life, I want
equally to warn against doing nothing! Many people
who go to church, either regularly or sporadically,
think that is all there is to it. They have not the faintest
idea that they need to encounter Jesus Christ in a personal way and decide whether or not they are going to
be his disciples.

It is a weakness in some mainline churches, and
often in strongly sacramental churches, implicitly to
encourage this misconception. Sacraments, churchgoing, and Bible reading can all be vehicles that take us to
Jesus: but they can all be stationary vehicles, getting us
nowhere, if we fail to emphasize that it is Jesus alone
who gives them vitality. It is not our job to pressurize a
friend, but it is our job to bring the person of the
incarnate, crucified, risen Jesus before him as clearly as
we can. If he pleads churchgoing as a means of evading
that encounter, we need gently to show that the church
is not something we go to: it is something we are—
limbs in the body of Christ. How can the limb have
any meaning, let alone life, if it is not joined up to the
head? Should Bible reading be put forward as an escape
route from commitment, you have only to open that
Bible to show how clearly it points to Jesus and the
need to surrender to him. Sometimes the sacraments,
instead of being a blessing, appear to be an obstacle, a
refuge from personal allegiance. If so, you need to
show how baptism (even received in infancy) is the
mark of the Christian, like the label on the bottle.
What hypocrisy if the liquid inside the bottle does not
correspond to the label! What hypocrisy if the baptized
are not plunged deep into the Christ whose name has
been marked upon them! And as for the Eucharist,
what an evangelistic meal it is: his body broken, his

blood shed—for your friend personally! Has he received the Savior as well as the consecrated elements? That is the issue.

The more images you use that embody response, the clearer it will be. Jesus says, "Come to me." Have we come yet? Jesus says, "I will come in." Has he been invited? He is the bridegroom; we are meant to be the bride. It can't happen until we say, "I will take you, for better, for worse, for richer, for poorer." That's when it all begins to become real.

So this ministry to people at the point of decision is a very sensitive thing. We must neither conceal the fact that a decision needs to be made nor lean on a friend to make that decision in our way at our convenience. We need to keep very close to our Master as we talk these things over with a friend. And that leads me to my final mistake. I know I often make it.

FAILING TO PRAY

It is such a relief to know that the whole work of imparting new life is God's task, not ours. But what a privilege it is to have a small part in it! That part is discharged by the life we live, the bridges we build, the explanations we give both of the good news and of our own discovery of it. But most of all, it is discharged by prayer. We have noted earlier that almost every new Christian is aware of someone who has been praying for him—usually a relative or a close friend. Prayer is not moving the hand that moves the world. It is humble cooperation with God in his purposes of good. And he often seems to limit himself to working only when his people pray. Prayer and evangelism are very closely intertwined.

But it is all very puzzling. Sometimes we pray for a dear one, and that person never responds. That may be because she is not willing to surrender to the Lord, and God respects her decision even when it is exercised against him. Sometimes we pray for one person, and another responds. That may be because God sees our attitude of humble cooperation with him, and uses it to bring light to a person who is ready for it but whom we had not thought of. Sometimes the answer comes years later: I once (and only once, I am ashamed to say) prayed for a man for fourteen years; and he came to faith through the ministry of African Christians when he was serving as a district officer in Kenya. The one thing I am sure about is that prayer is vital. If you press me as to why, I suppose it is because it expresses our inability to handle things on our own. God can work when that is our attitude. It is our supposed competence that gets in his way.

Everyone will have some favorite account of God working to bring someone to Christ, often quite unexpectedly. God is the great evangelist. He expects us to pray, to be ready, and to trust him: that is our part. I end with two stories that show his sovereign power and loving appeal at work. One comes from my own experience; the other I have just come across.

I was once on a mission at a college. During it I was plagued by the constant attacks of a virulently anti-Christian girl. On inquiry I found that she had begun by studying theology, but had suddenly become violently opposed to Christianity and took up philosophy —with great skill. At the end of the week she was still goading me, and I challenged her to come out for a drive in my car (fortunately, the days of political correctness had not arrived!) and tell me what was really bugging her. She did. And it concerned her sex life with her boyfriend. She knew what she was doing was wrong: she was not going to give up doing it, and so her Christian life went to pieces and she gave up theology. Well, she came back to the Lord that afternoon

with tears of repentance and joy. Imagine her amazement when her boyfriend told her that a similar thing
had happened to him that same day. He had been preparing a sermon (he was an ordinand) and before he
preached it, it struck him to the heart—and brought
him back in repentance and reinstatement. They are
now happily married! But the story stuck in my mind
as a lovely example that God is the supreme fisherman,
and he has his own time and methods for reaching
people: he simply allows us, sometimes, to take part.

The other story came from writer and teacher John
Drane. He was on the way to a conference on evangelism where he was to deliver the keynote address. Sit-
ting by him on the plane was a man who confided that
he had just walked out of his home for the last time,
because of marital stress: he was looking for satisfaction elsewhere.

John realized that he could hardly give that talk on
evangelism if he stayed silent! So he prayed a momen-
tary prayer for the right words to say and then blurted
out, "Do you know God?" The words were hardly out
of his mouth when he felt he had made a total mess of
it. But not at all. The man replied, "As a matter of fact I
don't, but if you know something of God, I'd like to
know more." A good conversation ensued, and three
weeks later John got a letter from the man saying that
he had been unable to forget the conversation, and
seeing a church door open, he went in and asked God
to intervene in his life. Well, in due course he returned
home, having nowhere else to go, and to his amazement received a warm welcome from his wife. The reason was astounding. She, too, had felt it was all over
when her husband had walked out. At the school gate,
she shared her feelings with a friend who invited her
along to a small prayer group she was about to attend.
She went, and was touched by their love and care for
her in her predicament. In fact, they prayed for her

husband at the very time John and he were talking in the plane. As a direct result of all this, husband and wife are reconciled and are Christians now, with a transformed family life and outlook.

Reflecting on it afterward, John realized that his part in it all was small but vital. He had given the man space to talk. He had listened. He had asked one question. And, basically, God had done the rest!

Such is the God we worship. He is very much the senior partner in this thrilling, if daunting, work of evangelism. He cares about people far more than we do. He will override our mistakes. He will work through us if we launch out humbly and sensitively among our friends and acquaintances, and if we trust him to use us, even us, as his partners in the most rewarding work this side of heaven.